That Choice, To Know, Will Be Yours

Aggregated Truth 2020

(In Support of President Donald J. Trump)

© 2020 David Caddell

(It will be helpful to have a magnifying glass handy for the sleuthing)

2

749

Matrix Movie Mind Control

Q !UW.yye1fxo 12 Feb 2018 - 9:50:26 AM

> **Anonymous** 12 Feb 2018 - 9:44:06 AM
>
> controlling the crops, controls the people
> (sheep)
> (might be reaching, but throwing it out there)

>>351343
Coincidence the Matrix (movie) grew people as a crop,
used for energy, and controlled their mind?
Sound familiar?
Wonder where they derived that idea from.
Now comes the 'conspiracy' label.
Deeper we go, the more unrealistic it all becomes.
The end won't be for everyone.
That choice, to know, will be yours.
Q

Origin of the Phrase, "Conspiracy Theory"

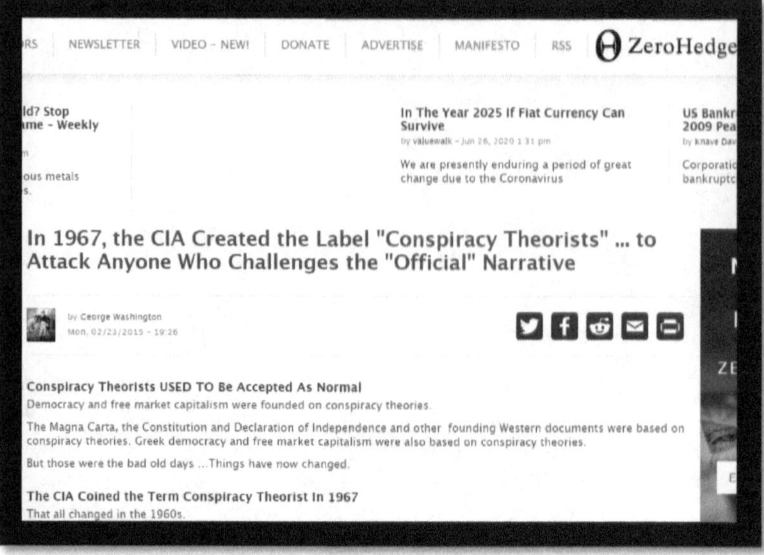

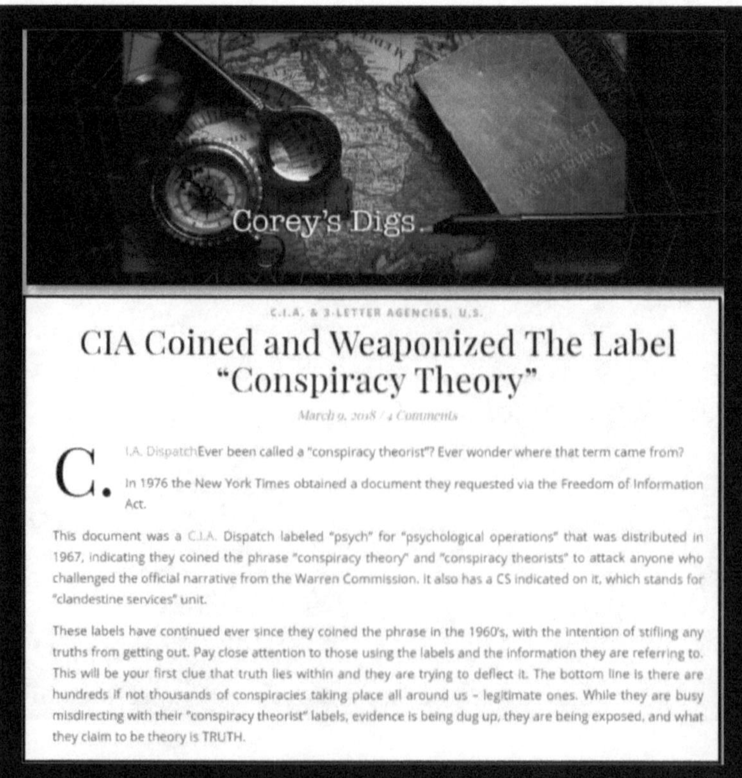

DISPATCH

PROCESSING ACTION

MARKED FOR INDEXING

X NO INDEXING REQUIRED

ONLY QUALIFIED DESK
CAN JUDGE INDEXING

TO
Chiefs, Certain Stations and Bases

INFO.

Document Number 1035-960

FROM
Chief, WOVIEW   for FOIA Review on   SEP 1976

SUBJECT
Countering Criticism of the Warren Report

ACTION REQUIRED - REFERENCES

PAUL H.   FOR OSWALD
PSYCH   FILE! 2 COPIES

THIS WAS PULLED TOGETHER BY NED BENNETT OF CA STAFF IN CLOSE CONJUNCTION WITH CI/R&A. WE FURNISHED MOST OF THE SOURCE MATERIAL, PROPOSED MANY OF THE THEMES, AND PROVIDED GENERAL "EXPERTISE" ON THE CASE. THE SPECIMEN ARTICLE WAS WRITTEN BY BENNETT.   G.E. Dough 28 JAN 1967

1. <u>Our Concern</u>. From the day of President Kennedy's assassination on, there has been speculation about the responsibility for his murder. Although this was stemmed for a time by the Warren Commission report (which appeared at the end of September 1964), various writers have now had time to scan the Commission's published report and documents for new pretexts for questioning, and there has been a new wave of books and articles criticizing the Commission's findings. In most cases the critics have speculated as to the existence of some kind of conspiracy, and often they have implied that the Commission itself was involved. Presumably as a result of the increasing challenge to the Warren Commission's Report, a public opinion poll recently indicated that 46% of the American public did not think that Oswald acted alone, while more than half of those polled thought that the Commission had left some questions unresolved. Doubtless polls abroad would show similar, or possibly more adverse, results.

2. This trend of opinion is a matter of concern to the U.S. government, including our organization. The members of the Warren Commission were naturally chosen for their integrity, experience, and prominence. They represented both major parties, and they and their staff were deliberately drawn from all sections of the country. Just because of the standing of the Commissioners, efforts to impugn their rectitude and wisdom tend to cast doubt on the whole leadership of American society. Moreover, there seems to be an increasing tendency to hint that President Johnson himself, as the one person who might be said to have benefited, was in some way responsible for the assassination. Innuendo of such seriousness affects not only the individual concerned, but also the whole reputation of the American government. Our organization itself is directly involved: among other facts, we contributed information to the investigation. Conspiracy theories have frequently thrown suspicion on our organization, for example by falsely alleging that Lee Harvey Oswald worked for us. The aim of this dispatch is to provide material for countering and discrediting the claims of the conspiracy theorists, so as to inhibit the circulation of such claims in other countries. Background information is supplied in a classified section and in a number of unclassified attachments.

3. <u>Action</u>. We do <u>not</u> recommend that discussion of the assassination question be initiated where it is not already taking place. <u>Where discussion is active</u>, however, addressees are requested:

CS COPY

201-289248

CROSS REFERENCE TO
ABSTRACT X INDEX
9 attachments h/w

DISPATCH SYMBOL AND NUMBER
BD 5847

DATE
4/1/67

1 - SECRET   *8 atts.*
8 - Unclassified

CLASSIFICATION
S̶E̶C̶R̶E̶T̶

HQS FILE NUMBER
DESTROY WHEN NO LONGER NEEDED

a. To discuss the publicity problem with liaison and friendly elite contacts (especially politicians and editors), pointing out that the Warren Commission made as thorough an investigation as humanly possible, that the charges of the critics are without serious foundation, and that further speculative discussion only plays into the hands of the opposition. Point out also that parts of the conspiracy talk appear to be deliberately generated by Communist propagandists. Urge them to use their influence to discourage unfounded and irresponsible speculation.

b. To employ propaganda assets to answer and refute the attacks of the critics. Book reviews and feature articles are particularly appropriate for this purpose. The unclassified attachments to this guidance should provide useful background material for passage to assets. Our play should point out, as applicable, that the critics are (i) wedded to theories adopted before the evidence was in, (ii) politically interested, (iii) financially interested, (iv) hasty and inaccurate in their research, or (v) infatuated with their own theories. In the course of discussions of the whole phenomenon of criticism, a useful strategy may be to single out Epstein's theory for attack, using the attached Fletcher Knebel article and Spectator piece for background. (Although Mark Lane's book is much less convincing than Epstein's and comes off badly where contested by knowledgeable critics, it is also much more difficult to answer as a whole, as one becomes lost in a morass of unrelated details.)

4. In private or media discussion not directed at any particular writer, or in attacking publications which may be yet forthcoming, the following arguments should be useful:

a. <u>No significant new evidence</u> has emerged which the Commission did not consider. The assassination is sometimes compared (e.g., by Joachim Joesten and Bertrand Russell) with the Dreyfus case; however, unlike that case, the attacks on the Warren Commission have produced no new evidence, no new culprits have been convincingly identified, and there is no agreement among the critics. (A better parallel, though an imperfect one, might be with the Reichstag fire of 1933, which some competent historians (Fritz Tobias, A.J.P. Taylor, D.C. Watt) now believe was set by Van der Lubbe on his own initiative, without acting for either Nazis or Communists; the Nazis tried to pin the blame on the Communists, but the latter have been much more successful in convincing the world that the Nazis were to blame.)

b. Critics usually overvalue particular items and ignore others. They tend to place more emphasis on the recollections of individual eyewitnesses (which are less reliable and more divergent -- and hence offer more hand-holds for criticism) and less on ballistic, autopsy, and photographic evidence. A close examination of the Commission's records will usually show that the conflicting eyewitness accounts are quoted out of context, or were discarded by the Commission for good and sufficient reason.

c. Conspiracy on the large scale often suggested would be impossible to conceal in the United States, esp. since informants could expect to receive large royalties, etc. Note that Robert Kennedy, Attorney General at the time and John F. Kennedy's brother, would be the last man to overlook or conceal any conspiracy. And as one reviewer pointed out, Congressman Gerald R. Ford would hardly have held his tongue for the sake of the Democratic administration, and Senator Russell would have had every political interest in exposing any misdeeds on the part of Chief Justice Warren. A conspirator moreover would hardly choose a location for a shooting where so much depended on conditions beyond his control: the route, the speed of the cars, the moving target, the risk that the assassin would be discovered. A group of wealthy conspirators could have arranged much more secure conditions.

d. Critics have often been enticed by a form of intellectual pride: they light on some theory and fall in love with it; they also scoff at the Commission because it did not always answer every question with a flat decision one way or the other. Actually, the make-up of the Commission and its staff was an excellent safeguard against over-commitment to any one theory, or against the illicit transformation of probabilities into certainties.

Here are some pretty obvious examples of conspiracy *"theories"*:

The Detroit News EXTRA

THE HOME NEWSPAPER

FRIDAY, NOVEMBER 22, 1963 — 91st YEAR, NO. 92 — 4 SECTIONS—44 PAGES — TEN CENTS

KENNEDY DEAD

Slain in Car by Dallas Assassin

Romney Indicates Doubts About Backing Goldwater

Ford Buys Lions; Fight Threatened

Board Asks Talks With Teachers

Trooper Halted, Released

Was Stopped by Police as He Fled Bank Raid

TROOPER-BANDIT ANDY I. SALEOVIC II

PRESIDENT KENNEDY

Susan Rice makes claim Russians could be behind violent George Floyd demonstrations

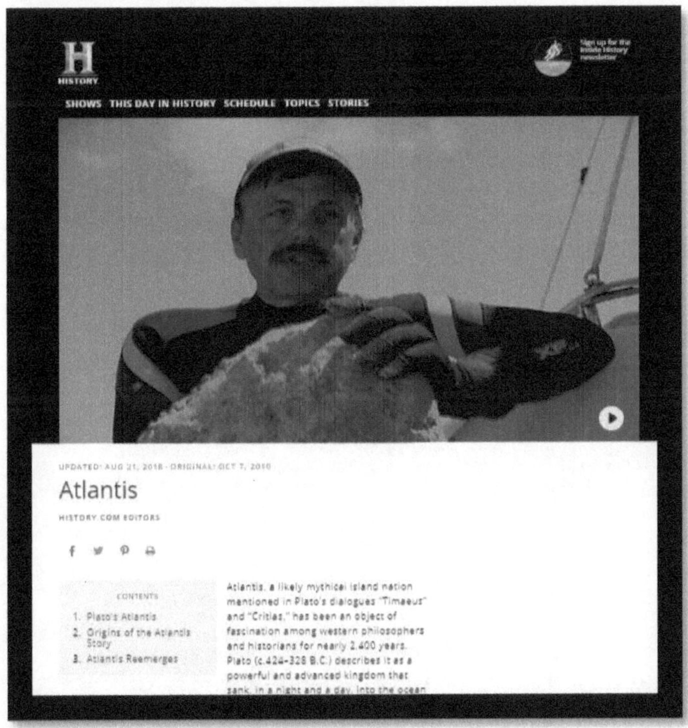

Here are some examples of conspiracy *"facts"*:

On Reddit

On October 27th, 2017, Redditor TheLoneGreyWolf submitted a post asking "What is the most interesting thing you've found in the JFK files?" to the /r/AskReddit[2] subreddit, where it received upwards of 30,700 points (91% upvoted) and 6,200 comments. In the comments section, top-voted comments discussed the mystery of journalist Dorothy Kilgallen's death, which remained classified. Additionally, an unclassified document discussed the KGB possessing evidence that President Lyndon B. Johnson was responsible for the assassination (shown below).

> On September 16, 1965, this same source reported that the KGB Residency in New York City received instructions approximately September 16, 1965, from KGB headquarters in Moscow to develop all possible information concerning President Lyndon B. Johnson's character, background, personal friends, family, and from which quarters he derives his support in his position as President of the United States. Our source added that in the instructions from Moscow, it was indicated that "now" the KGB was in possession of data purporting to indicate President Johnson was responsible for the assassination of the late President John F. Kennedy. KGB headquarters indicated that in view of this information, it was necessary for the Soviet Government to know the existing personal relationship between President Johnson and the Kennedy family, particularly that between President Johnson and Robert and "Ted" Kennedy.

Redditor cheezzy4ever posted a link to a CIA document discussing a report that Adolf Hitler had been seen alive in Colombia after World War II.[3] Others discussed the reaction of the Soviet Union to the assassination, which appeared to indicate they had no involvement.

American Thinker

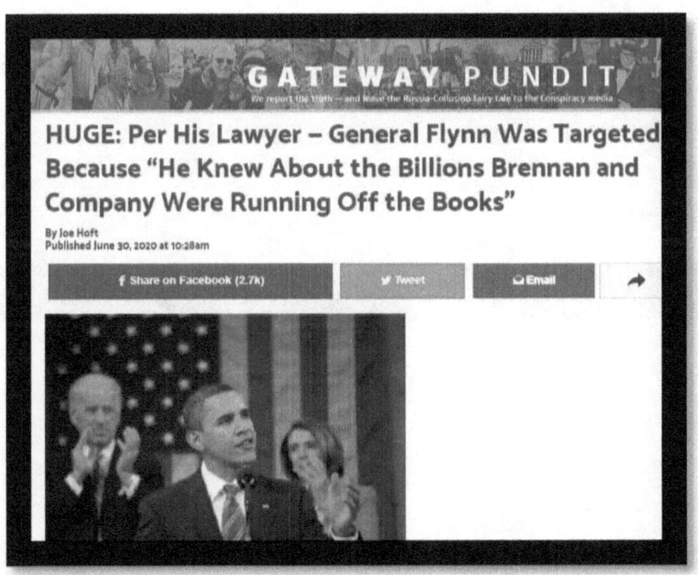

Free Republic
Browse · Search

News/Activism
Topics · Post Article

Skip to comments.

Seth Rich Refuses to Stay Buried
American Thinker.com ^ | May 11, 2020 | Jack Cashill

Posted on 5/11/2020, 6:25:07 AM by Kaslin

"I am reliably informed that the NSA or its partners intercepted at least some of the communications between Mr. Rich and Wikileaks," wrote attorney Ty Clevenger in a startling letter last week to Richard Grennell, Interim Director of National Intelligence.

Clevenger represents Ed Butowsky, a high-profile author and financial adviser who dared to ask questions about the late Seth Rich and was sued for his troubles.

The known facts of Rich's still unsolved murder were largely established within hours by the local media: "A 27-year-old man who worked for the Democratic National Committee was shot and killed as he walked home early Sunday in the Bloomingdale neighborhood of Northwest Washington, D.C.," NBC Washington reported.

The shooting occurred at 4:19 a.m. on Sunday, July 10, 2016. "There had been a struggle," said Seth's mother, Mary Rich. "His hands were bruised, his knees are bruised, his face is bruised, and yet he had two shots to his back, and yet they never took anything." She added, "They took his life for literally no reason."

In the real world, most killers have a reason. Those who fire two shots and take nothing from the victim always do. In the major newsrooms, journalists have been perversely keen on not knowing what this reason was. In the years since the shooting, they have offered little useful information beyond the account above.

Butowsky was much more curious. The woman who stirred his curiosity was Ellen Ratner, a veteran TV news analyst. On the day after the 2016 presidential election, Ratner participated in a videotaped panel discussion at Embry-Riddle University.

"I spent three hours with Julian Assange on Saturday at the Ecuadorian Embassy in London," said Ratner with a curious lack of emphasis.

(Excerpt) Read more at americanthinker.com ...

BREAKING: The Case Against General Michael Flynn Has Officially Been Dismissed

Katie Pavlich | @KatiePavlich | Posted: Jun 24, 2020 10:50 AM

Share

THE UNITED STATES
DEPARTMENT of JUSTICE

ABOUT   OUR AGENCY   PRIORITIES   NEWS   RESOURCES   CAREE

Home » Office of Public Affairs » News

JUSTICE NEWS

Department of Justice

Office of Public Affairs

FOR IMMEDIATE RELEASE

Monday, June 29, 2020

Chinese National Guilty of Laundering Millions for Mexican Drug Cartels

A Chinese national pleaded guilty today to conspiracy to commit money laundering in connection with laundering more than $4 million in drug proceeds generated by large-scale cocaine trafficking in the United States.

President Trump arriving on Friday in Morristown, N.J. Anna Moneymaker/The New York Times

By Michael Crowley

Aug. 10, 2019

Why this Blog?   Prepped and Prepared
Everything Nuke 2Day
Health, Food and Farms
Food/Beef Prices To Soar in CA ▾
Mind Controlling Our Children
Revisionist History   Astrology
Naturally Healing All Cancers With Hemp Oil
Teenage News and Views ▾
Hell No! to Mandatory Forced Vaccinations
Jesuits; Rulers of Evil   The Lighter Side
Best of Alt-News Links   Never Give Up
There is NO More Important Subject Matter in Our Time Than This
Other Author Weblinks   Contact   About

TABU; Towards A Better Understanding

To Awaken, To Alert, To Inform

The Manufactured Invention of the Beatles, Stones, Grateful Dead and the Birth of Rock n' Roll by the Tavistock Institute; A Jesuit Corporation.

"The fact that "The Beatles" had their music and lyrics written for them by Theo Adorno was concealed from public view." John Coleman, former MI6 agent.

Paul and John giving Masonic Illuminate Hand signals on Yellow Submarine album cover. Paul with the "**666**" hand sign, John with the **Horned Hand**

****

****

Stones Logo: Sticking your tongue out against the Establishment

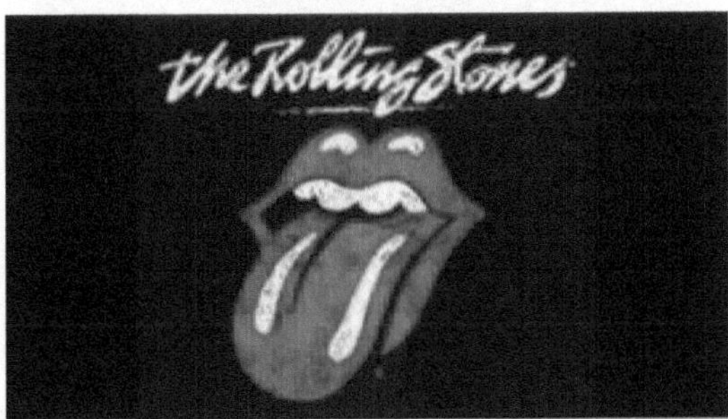

"**The Rolling Stones were mastered by a Order of Malta member by** the name of Prince Rupert Loewenstein who sponsored the '*Sympathy for the Devil*' track back in 1968. This Prince was also a member of the very powerful <u>Sacred Military Constantinian Order of St George</u> which is close in power to the <u>Equestrian Order of the Holy Sepulchre of Jerusalem</u>, both being higher than the Order of Malta. (The Order of Malta, SMOM, is the military arm of the Vatican <u>here</u>)

It was called the "British Invasion" . The 60's began a time of "question authority", grow your hair long, hippies and flower power and morphed in with the Anti War gang of "hell no we won't go!"

All by design, all by planning to mind control and manipulate what the Baby Boomer (Doomer) generation thought, the language and slang used and the behavior control of the masses.

Yes, it is interesting to note that the Tavistock Institute of Human Relation, as well as, it's child organization: The Stanford Research Institute, developed The Grateful Dead, among other things.
You can see that Alan Trist, a social engineer for the Tavistock Institute, became the shadow manager of the Dead. His father, Eric Trist, was one of the principle founding members of Tavistock.

It was part of the development of a dynamic psychological warfare model to be used on foreign and domestic populations, modeled, ultimately, on the Lord Gordon Riots in London and the Jacobin Terror of the French Revolution. The purpose was to mobilize mobs in ideological opposition to the state, as a mass destabilization operation. (Source)

Rebellion against society, let your hair grow...turn on, tune out, as millions of tabs of LSD appeared into the hippie scene from CIA laboratories and promotion provided by Harvard CIA asset, Timothy Leary and distribution aided by the likes of the Grateful Dead. (source)

The men buried in the think tanks and research institutions, whose names and faces are still not known to but a few people, made sure that the press played its part. Conversely, the media's important role in not exposing the power behind the future cultural shocks made certain that the source of the crisis was never identified.

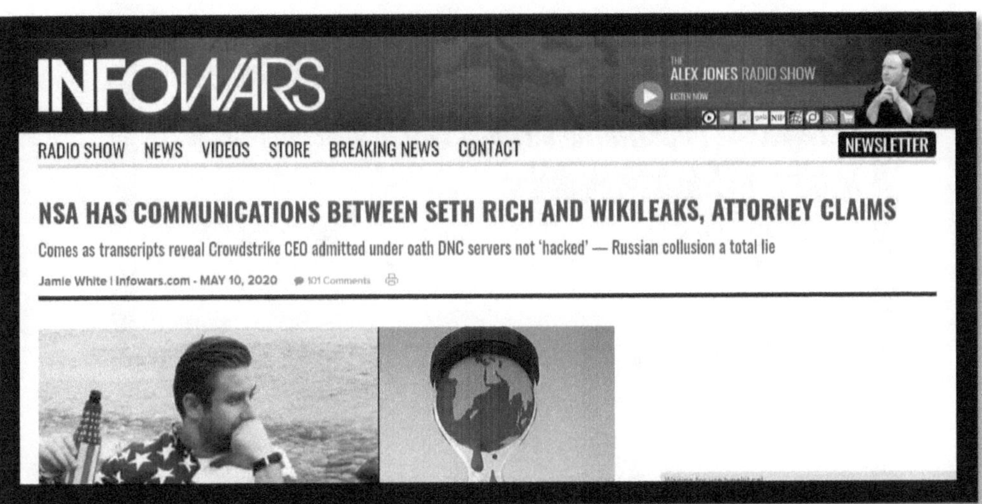

INFOWARS

THE ALEX JONES RADIO SHOW

LISTEN NOW

RADIO SHOW NEWS VIDEOS STORE BREAKING NEWS CONTACT NEWSLETTER

NSA HAS COMMUNICATIONS BETWEEN SETH RICH AND WIKILEAKS, ATTORNEY CLAIMS

Comes as transcripts reveal Crowdstrike CEO admitted under oath DNC servers not 'hacked' — Russian collusion a total lie

Jamie White | Infowars.com - MAY 10, 2020 101 Comments

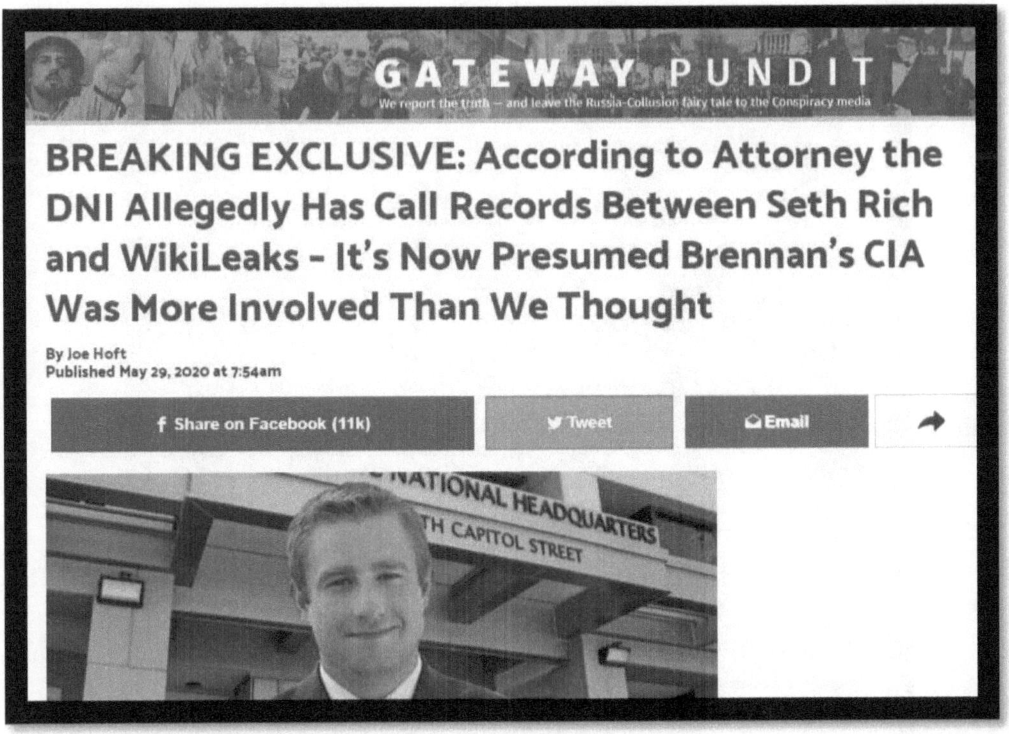

GATEWAY PUNDIT

We report the truth – and leave the Russia-Collusion fairy tale to the Conspiracy media

BREAKING EXCLUSIVE: According to Attorney the DNI Allegedly Has Call Records Between Seth Rich and WikiLeaks – It's Now Presumed Brennan's CIA Was More Involved Than We Thought

By Joe Hoft
Published May 29, 2020 at 7:54am

Share on Facebook (11k) Tweet Email

NATIONAL HEADQUARTERS
TH CAPITOL STREET

BEAST INSIDE Dig Deeper JOIN NOW

DAILY BEAST

CROSSWORD

CORONAVIRUS CHEAT SHEET POLITICS ENTERTAINMENT WORLD NEWS HALF FULL CULTURE U.S. NEWS SCO

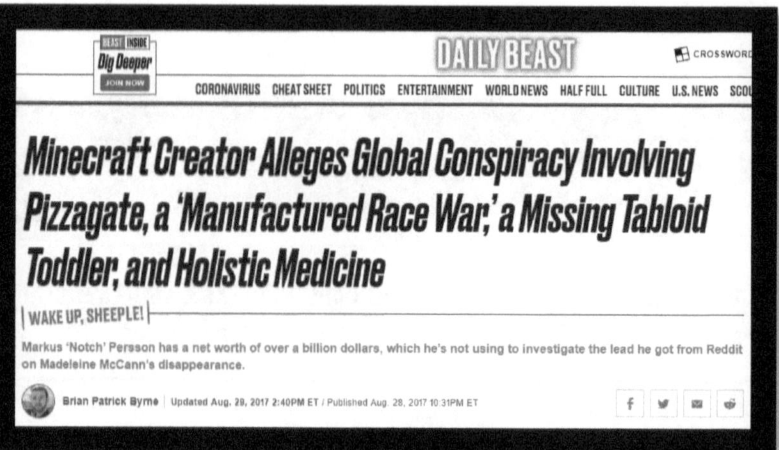

Minecraft Creator Alleges Global Conspiracy Involving Pizzagate, a 'Manufactured Race War,' a Missing Tabloid Toddler, and Holistic Medicine

WAKE UP, SHEEPLE!

Markus 'Notch' Persson has a net worth of over a billion dollars, which he's not using to investigate the lead he got from Reddit on Madeleine McCann's disappearance.

Brian Patrick Byrne | Updated Aug. 29, 2017 2:40PM ET / Published Aug. 28, 2017 10:31PM ET

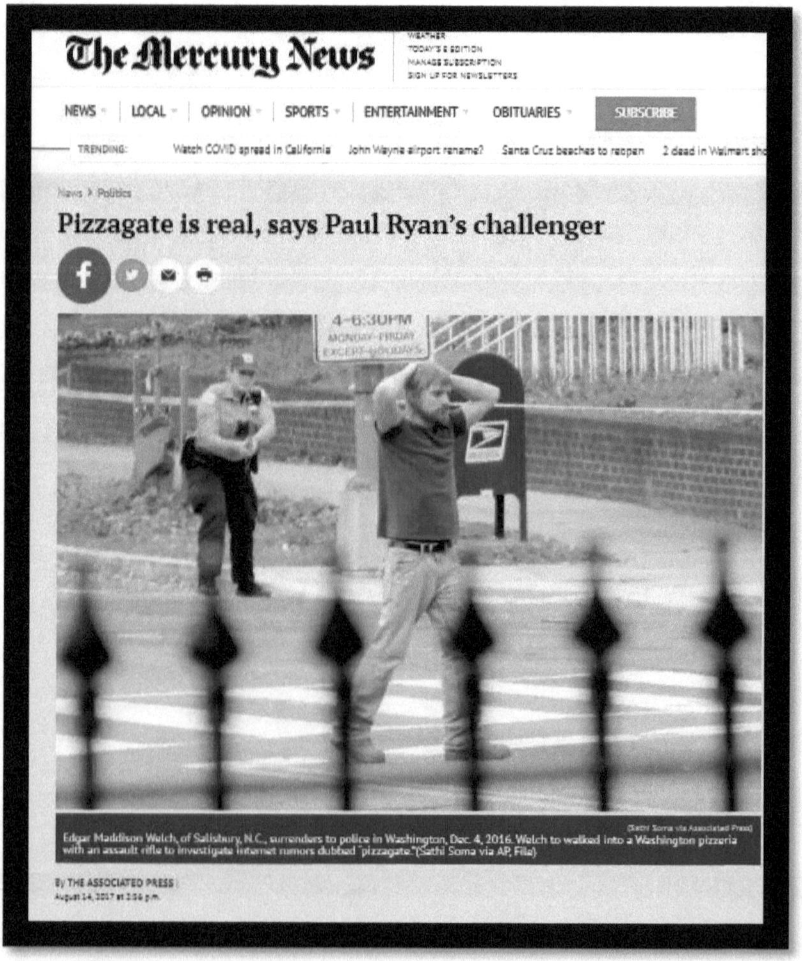

The Mercury News

WEATHER
TODAY'S E-EDITION
MANAGE SUBSCRIPTION
SIGN UP FOR NEWSLETTERS

NEWS LOCAL OPINION SPORTS ENTERTAINMENT OBITUARIES SUBSCRIBE

TRENDING: Watch COVID spread in California John Wayne airport rename? Santa Cruz beaches to reopen 2 dead in Walmart sh

News > Politics

Pizzagate is real, says Paul Ryan's challenger

(Sathi Soma via Associated Press)

Edgar Maddison Welch, of Salisbury, N.C., surrenders to police in Washington, Dec. 4, 2016. Welch to walked into a Washington pizzeria with an assault rifle to investigate internet rumors dubbed "pizzagate."(Sathi Soma via AP, File)

By THE ASSOCIATED PRESS |
August 14, 2017 at 3:56 p.m.

► MEGA AGENCY
FOX NEWS channel
► DANIEL HALPER | "A CONVENIENT DEATH" AUTHOR
BOOK CLAIMS CLINTON HAD AN AFFAIR WITH MAXWELL
AIRLINES FROM LAYING OFF OR CUTTING EMPLOYEE SALARIES UNTIL AFTER SEPT 30   FOX NEWS   NY TI

FOX NEWS channel
FBI NOTES: OBAMA WANTED "THE RIGHT PEOPLE ON IT"
Watters' World
SCOURAGE VOTING AND INCREASING ITS ENFORCEMENT CAPACITY TO REMOVE FALSE CLAIMS ABOUT LOC

OBAMA KNEW
FOX NEWS friends FIRST
3:14 CT
ES...   WHITE HOUSE SAID TRUMP SPOKE WITH PUTIN "TO COMMEMORATE AND REFLECT UPON T

Bill Clinton's Serbian War Atrocities Exposed In New Indictment

by **Tyler Durden**
Tue, 06/30/2020 – 22:45

Authored by Jim Bovard via The Libertarian Institute,

President Bill Clinton's favorite freedom fighter **just got indicted for mass murder, torture, kidnapping, and other crimes against humanity**. In 1999, the Clinton administration launched a 78-day bombing campaign that killed up to 1500 civilians in Serbia and Kosovo in what the American media proudly portrayed as a crusade against ethnic bias. That war, like most of the pretenses of U.S. foreign policy, was always a sham.

The Unnecessary Words

All of those unnecessary words that exist in the shadowy closets of our minds like dust-covered wax figures of celebrities that nobody wants to admit remembering anymore – Those words that conjure concepts we dare not admit everyone knows yet never discusses for fear of a terrifying acknowledgment of the truth – Yet again, haven't we thought for a second what might have been happening "above ground" while our "heads have been planted in the sand" with our exposed asses sticking in the air asking to get blown clean off? It is time for that now, before our asses get blown clean off.

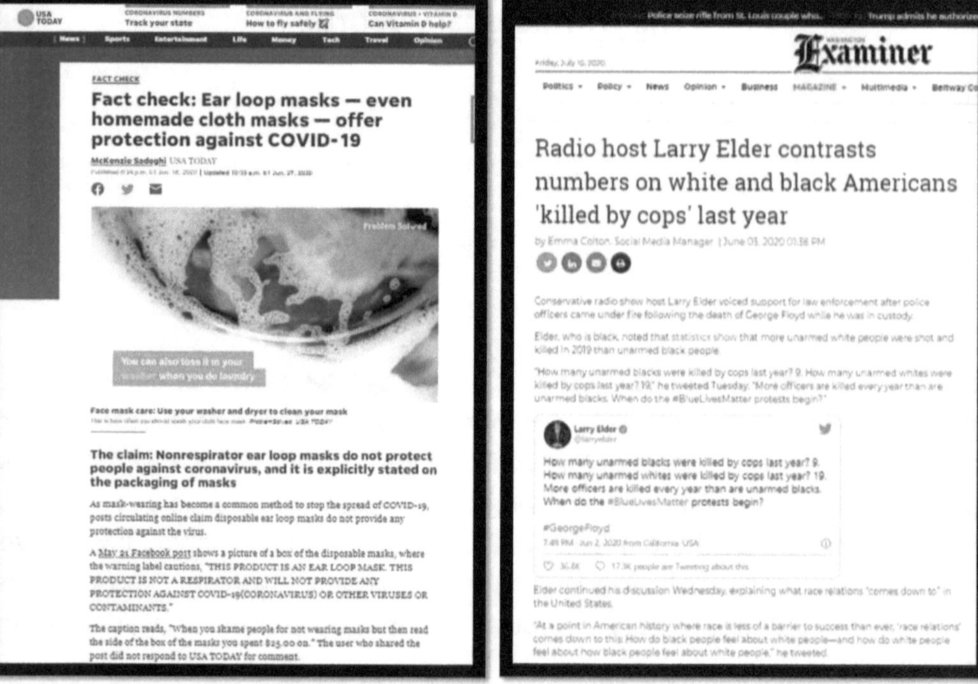

USA TODAY

FACT CHECK

Fact check: Ear loop masks — even homemade cloth masks — offer protection against COVID-19

McKenzie Sadeghi USA TODAY

Face mask care: Use your washer and dryer to clean your mask
This is how often you should wash your cloth face mask. *ProblemSolved, USA TODAY*

The claim: Nonrespirator ear loop masks do not protect people against coronavirus, and it is explicitly stated on the packaging of masks

As mask-wearing has become a common method to stop the spread of COVID-19, posts circulating online claim disposable ear loop masks do not provide any protection against the virus.

A May 21 Facebook post shows a picture of a box of the disposable masks, where the warning label cautions, "THIS PRODUCT IS AN EAR LOOP MASK. THIS PRODUCT IS NOT A RESPIRATOR AND WILL NOT PROVIDE ANY PROTECTION AGAINST COVID-19(CORONAVIRUS) OR OTHER VIRUSES OR CONTAMINANTS."

The caption reads, "When you shame people for not wearing masks but then read the side of the box of the masks you spent $25.00 on." The user who shared the post did not respond to USA TODAY for comment.

Examiner

Friday, July 10, 2020

Radio host Larry Elder contrasts numbers on white and black Americans 'killed by cops' last year

by Emma Colton, Social Media Manager | June 03, 2020 01:38 PM

Conservative radio show host Larry Elder voiced support for law enforcement after police officers came under fire following the death of George Floyd while he was in custody.

Elder, who is black, noted that statistics show that more unarmed white people were shot and killed in 2019 than unarmed black people.

"How many unarmed blacks were killed by cops last year? 9. How many unarmed whites were killed by cops last year? 19," he tweeted Tuesday. "More officers are killed every year than are unarmed blacks. When do the #BlueLivesMatter protests begin?"

Elder continued his discussion Wednesday, explaining what race relations "comes down to" in the United States.

"At a point in American history where race is less of a barrier to success than ever, 'race relations' comes down to this: How do black people feel about white people—and how do white people feel about how black people feel about white people," he tweeted.

OPINION *This piece expresses the views of its author(s), separate from those of this publication.*

There is no epidemic of fatal police shootings against unarmed Black Americans

Ideally officers would never need to take anyone's life. But the data on police killings doesn't support reducing or abolishing law enforcement.

Heather Mac Donald Opinion contributor

Published 5:15 a.m. ET Jul. 3, 2020 | Updated 10:29 a.m. ET Jul. 6, 2020

Surveillance: George Floyd's first contact with police
Surveillance video in Minneapolis shows the final moments of George Floyd's police interaction. USA TODAY

The video of George Floyd's tragic death under the knee of a Minneapolis police officer has led many to ask whether it represents the tip of an iceberg of police brutality. For centuries, United States law enforcement was interwoven with slavery and segregation, and that memory cannot be easily erased. But the evidence does not support the charge that biased police are systematically killing Black Americans in fatal shootings.

Much of modern policing is driven by crime data and community demands for help. The African American community tends to be policed more heavily, because that is where people are disproportionately hurt by violent street crime. In New York City in 2018, 73% of shooting victims were Black, though Black residents comprise only 24% of the city's population.

FOX NEWS
U.S. World Opinion Politics Entertainment Business Lifestyle TV Fox Nation Listen More
Hot Topics
FOX NEWS FLASH · Published March 31
Surgeon general: Data doesn't back up wearing masks in public amid coronavirus pandemic
By Talia Kaplan | Fox News
Fox News

Support The Guardian
Available for everyone, funded by readers
Contribute →
Subscribe →
Search jobs
Sign in
Search
US edition
The Guardian
News   Opinion   Sport   Culture   Lifestyle   More
World ▶ Europe US Americas Asia Australia Middle East Africa Inequality Global development
World Health Organization
This article is more than 3 months old
Face masks cannot stop healthy people getting Covid-19, says WHO
Organisation's evidence review shows wearing mask outside does not prevent infection
+ Coronavirus – latest updates
+ See all our coronavirus coverage
Ian Sample Science editor
Read The Guardian without interruption on all your devices
Subscribe now
most viewed in US
New York's hungry

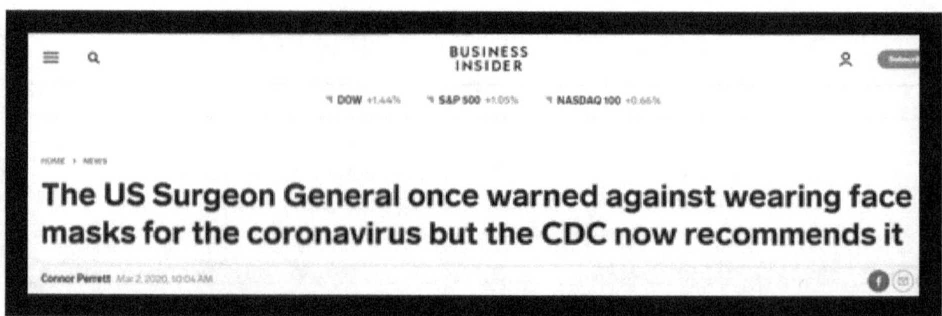

BUSINESS INSIDER
DOW +1.44%   S&P 500 +1.05%   NASDAQ 100 +0.66%
HOME ▸ NEWS
The US Surgeon General once warned against wearing face masks for the coronavirus but the CDC now recommends it
Connor Perrett Mar 2, 2020, 10:04 AM

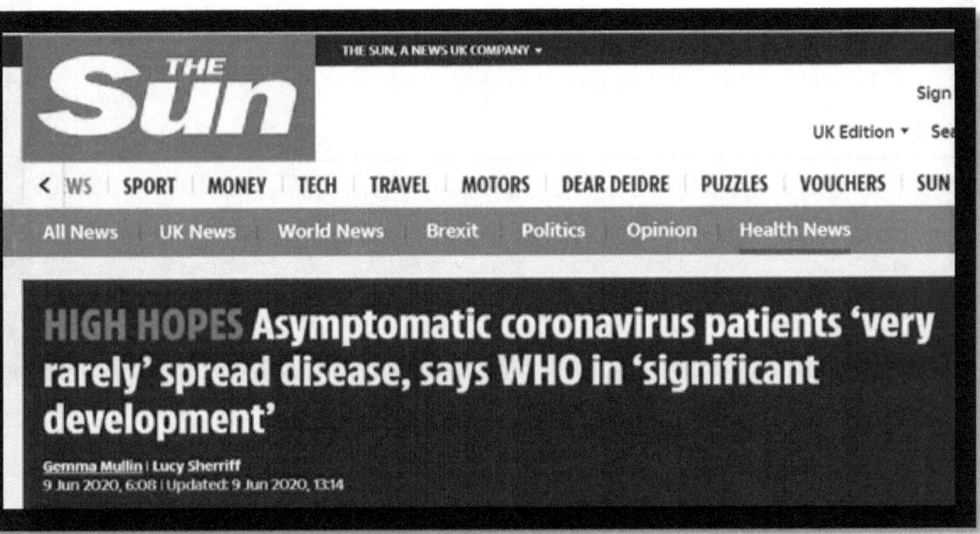

THE SUN, A NEWS UK COMPANY
THE Sun
Sign
UK Edition
Sea
NEWS | SPORT | MONEY | TECH | TRAVEL | MOTORS | DEAR DEIDRE | PUZZLES | VOUCHERS | SUN
All News | UK News | World News | Brexit | Politics | Opinion | Health News
HIGH HOPES Asymptomatic coronavirus patients 'very rarely' spread disease, says WHO in 'significant development'
Gemma Mullin | Lucy Sherriff
9 Jun 2020, 6:08 | Updated: 9 Jun 2020, 13:14

CLICK ON DETROIT
71°F
JOIN INSI
NEWS SPORTS FEATURES LIVE IN THE D ANN ARBOR WEATHER TRAFFIC NEWSLETTERS CONTAC
WEATHER ALERT 3 warnings, 7 watches and 3 advisories in effect for 7 counties in the area
SHOW
LOCAL NEWS
Frank McGeorge, MD, Local 4's Good Health Medical Expert
Published: June 10, 2020, 6:51 am
Tags: Asymptomatic, Coronavirus, Health, News, Good Health, COVID-19, Metro Detroit, World Health Organization, CDC, Pandemic, Contracting Virus, Virus
Sign up for our Newsletters
Enter your email here
WHO walks back statement on asymptomatic spread of coronavirus
Statement contradicts CDC guidance

Asymptomatic Infected Rarely Spread COVID-19

Well, well. The World Health Organization now says asymptomatic people with COVID infection rarely spread the disease. From the CNBC story:

> Coronavirus patients who don't have any symptoms aren't driving the spread of the virus, World Health Organization officials said Monday, casting doubt on concerns by some researchers that the virus could be difficult to contain due to asymptomatic infections. . . .

> "From the data we have, it still seems to be rare that an asymptomatic person actually transmits onward to a secondary individual," Dr. Maria Van Kerkhove, head of WHO's emerging diseases and zoonosis unit, said at a news briefing from the United Nations agency's Geneva headquarters. "It's very rare."

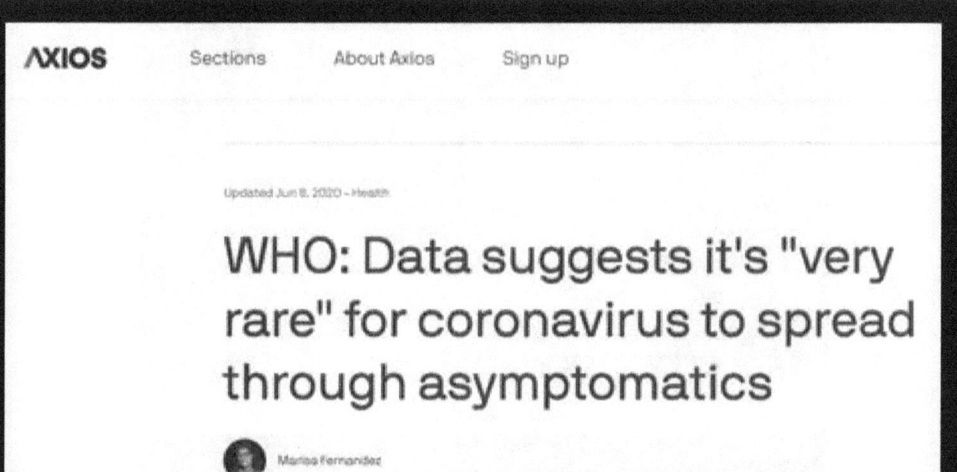

AXIOS
Sections   About Axios   Sign up
Updated Jun 8, 2020 – Health
WHO: Data suggests it's "very rare" for coronavirus to spread through asymptomatics
Marisa Fernandez

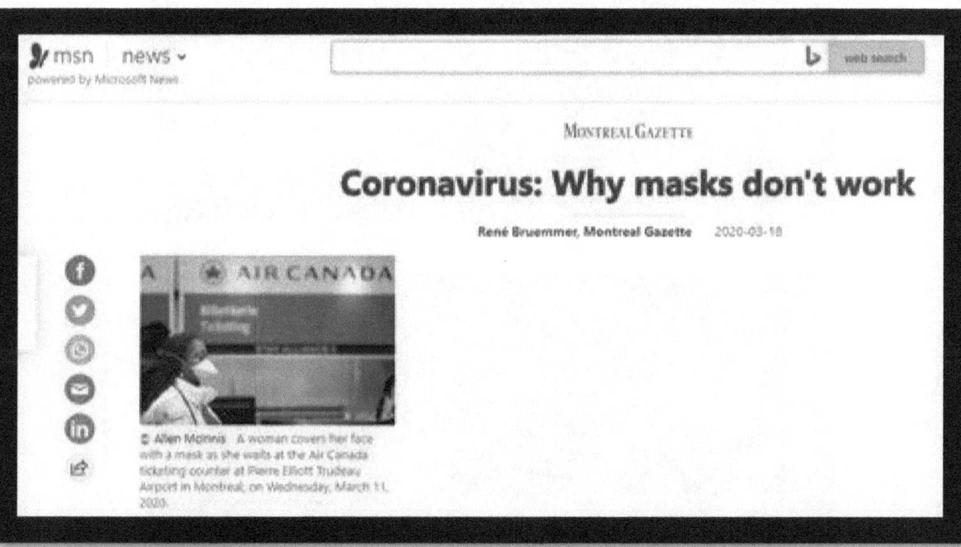

msn   news
powered by Microsoft News
web search
MONTREAL GAZETTE
Coronavirus: Why masks don't work
René Bruemmer, Montreal Gazette   2020-03-18
AIR CANADA
© Allen McInnis   A woman covers her face with a mask as she waits at the Air Canada ticketing counter at Pierre Elliott Trudeau Airport in Montreal, on Wednesday, March 11, 2020.

Newsmax health

Home : Health News

Tags: Coronavirus | Health Topics | face mask | oxygen

Does Wearing a Face Mask Increase CO2 Levels?

A park ranger patrols the Grand Canyon after it partially reopened from coronavirus closures. (Mario Tama/Getty Images)

By Lynn Allison | Wednesday, 27 May 2020 12:33 PM

f Share | Like | Email Article | Comment | Contact | Print | A A

Health officials urge us to wear face masks in public to reduce the risk of infection from COVID-19. But many people complain that wearing a mask for a prolonged period of time makes them feel faint and dizzy.

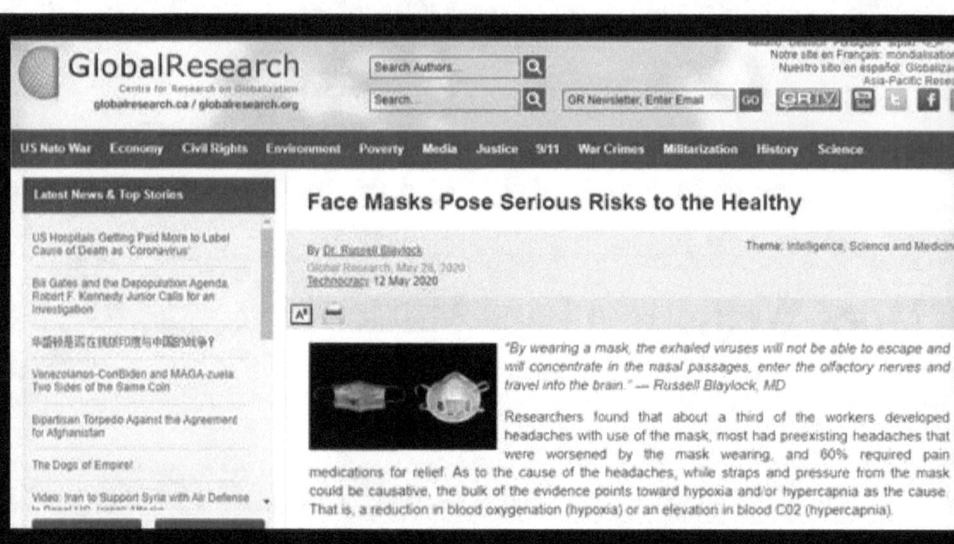

GlobalResearch
Centre for Research on Globalization
globalresearch.ca / globalresearch.org
Search Authors...
Search.
GR Newsletter, Enter Email
GO
GRTV
Notre site en Français: mondialisation
Nuestro sitio en español: Globalizac
Asia-Pacific Resea
US Nato War   Economy   Civil Rights   Environment   Poverty   Media   Justice   9/11   War Crimes   Militarization   History   Science
Latest News & Top Stories
US Hospitals Getting Paid More to Label Cause of Death as 'Coronavirus'
Bill Gates and the Depopulation Agenda. Robert F. Kennedy Junior Calls for an Investigation
半霉特是否在策划印度与中国的战争？
Venezolanos-ConBiden and MAGA-zuela Two Sides of the Same Coin
Bipartisan Torpedo Against the Agreement for Afghanistan
The Dogs of Empire!
Video: Iran to Support Syria with Air Defense
Face Masks Pose Serious Risks to the Healthy
By Dr. Russell Blaylock
Global Research, May 26, 2020
Technocracy 12 May 2020
Theme: Intelligence, Science and Medicine
"By wearing a mask, the exhaled viruses will not be able to escape and will concentrate in the nasal passages, enter the olfactory nerves and travel into the brain." — Russell Blaylock, MD
Researchers found that about a third of the workers developed headaches with use of the mask, most had preexisting headaches that were worsened by the mask wearing, and 60% required pain medications for relief. As to the cause of the headaches, while straps and pressure from the mask could be causative, the bulk of the evidence points toward hypoxia and/or hypercapnia as the cause. That is, a reduction in blood oxygenation (hypoxia) or an elevation in blood CO2 (hypercapnia).

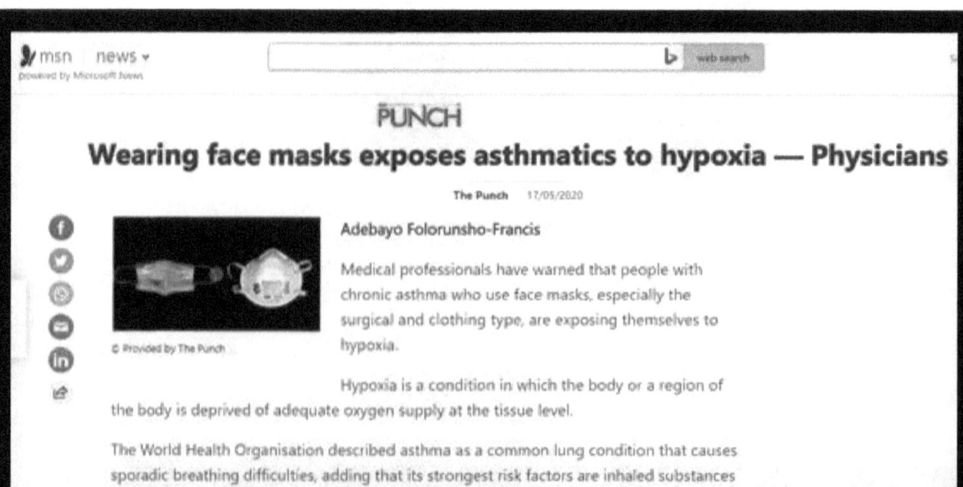

msn   news ▾
powered by Microsoft News
web search
PUNCH
Wearing face masks exposes asthmatics to hypoxia — Physicians
The Punch   17/05/2020
© Provided by The Punch
Adebayo Folorunsho-Francis
Medical professionals have warned that people with chronic asthma who use face masks, especially the surgical and clothing type, are exposing themselves to hypoxia.
Hypoxia is a condition in which the body or a region of the body is deprived of adequate oxygen supply at the tissue level.
The World Health Organisation described asthma as a common lung condition that causes sporadic breathing difficulties, adding that its strongest risk factors are inhaled substances and particles that may provoke allergic reactions or irritate the airways.

CHINA INSIDER
HONG KONG
National Security Law Impacts Hong Kong's Press Freedom

CHINA INSIDER
HONG KONG
National Security Law Impacts Hong Kong's Press Freedom

CHINA INSIDER
HONG KONG
National Security Law Impacts Hong Kong's Press Freedom

FCC Statement Condemning Further Violence Against Journalists Covering the Hong Kong Protests

The Foreign Correspondents' Club of Hong Kong expresses its deep concern over multiple reports of police violence on Sept. 28 and Sept. 29 against journalists covering the Hong Kong protests.

They include a report of a serious injury to an Indonesian journalist working for a Hong Kong-based publication who was shot in the face by a police officer using a non-lethal round. Footage from the incident shows she was clearly identified as a journalist and that the police officer fired a parting shot from only a few meters away.

The Human Rights Press Awards are run by the FCC, Amnesty International Hong Kong, and the Hong Kong Journalists Association. The 24th annual awards were announced on May 6, 2020. See the winners here.

2608

The Envelopes at the GHWB Funeral Contained Q's Promise to Counter

Q !!mG7VJxZNCl 12 Dec 2018 – 4:43:33 PM

Anonymous 12 Dec 2018 – 4:43:11 PM

>>4280189
What were in the envelopes ???

>>4280212
Our promise to 'counter'.
Q

2553

President Trump Risked Everything to Fight For & Defend We, the PEOPLE

Q !!mG7VJxZNCl 5 Dec 2018 – 11:27:19 AM

Anonymous 5 Dec 2018 – 10:56:46 AM

Screen Shot 2018-12-05 at 9.53.35 AM.png

POTUS FLOTUS not participating in this evil.

>>4166910
One man, who gave up everything, risking his life (himself/family), to fight for & defend, We, the PEOPLE.
Bait expends ammunition.
EVIL has no place here.
Q

3805

POTUS References George Washington and American Patriots Victory in Trenton, New Jersey (Q Proof)

Q !!Hs1Jq13jV6 28 Jan 2020 – 7:10:53 PM

https://twitter.com/PatriotsDontSlp/status/122 2337763984510977

THE BEST IS YET TO COME!
Q

2867

Motorcade Honk Referenced in Q Drop 1691

Q !!mG7VJxZNCI 22 Feb 2019 – 10:07:39 AM

https://www.youtube.com/watch?v=cI51wZVdwYA

Are we having fun yet?
The best is yet to come.
Q

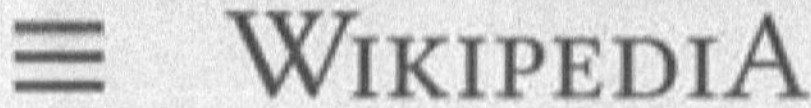

Through the Looking-Glass

For other uses, see Through the Looking Glass (disambiguation).

Through the Looking-Glass, and What Alice Found There (also known as **Alice Through the Looking-Glass** or simply **Through the Looking-Glass**) is an 1871 novel[1] by Lewis Carroll and the sequel to *Alice's Adventures in Wonderland* (1865). Alice again enters a fantastical world, this time by climbing through a mirror into the world that she can see beyond it. There she finds that, just like a reflection, everything is reversed, including logic (e.g. running helps you remain stationary, walking away from something brings you towards it, chessmen are alive, nursery rhyme characters exist, etc.)

u/misscloud · Jul 6, 2020

Former Reddit CEO Ellen K. Pao posted on Twitter a few hours ago that she was at a party with Ghislaine Maxwell and everyone there knew Maxwell trafficked underage girls for sex. And no one did anything about it. She deleted the post, set her account to private, and is blocking everyone who shares.

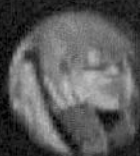

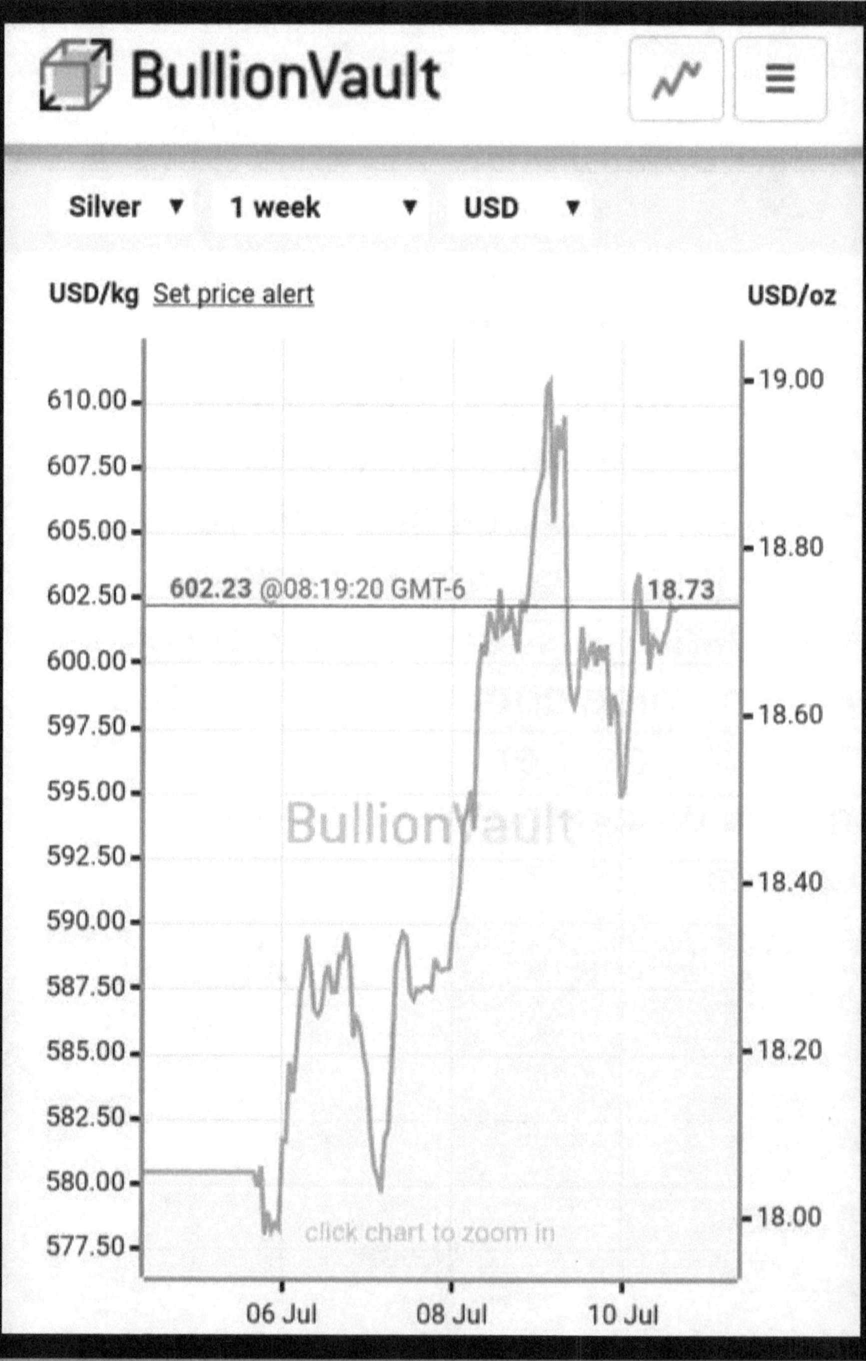

BullionVault
Silver ▼   1 week   ▼   USD ▼
USD/kg   Set price alert
USD/oz
610.00
607.50
605.00
602.50   602.23 @08:19:20 GMT-6   18.73
600.00
597.50
595.00
592.50
590.00
587.50
585.00
582.50
580.00
577.50
19.00
18.80
18.60
18.40
18.20
18.00
BullionVault
click chart to zoom in
06 Jul   08 Jul   10 Jul

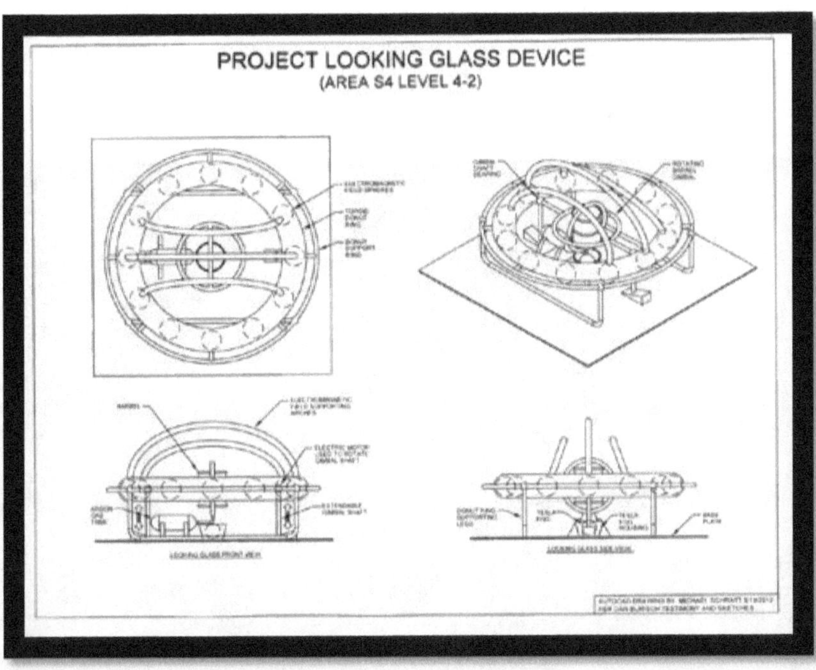

PROJECT LOOKING GLASS DEVICE
(AREA S4 LEVEL 4-2)

Jason
@jasonlight73

Replying to @LisaMei62

Did you see this? Who is this at the Pennsylvania Trump/Lou Barletta Rally? #MAGA #Qanon

4:51 PM · 10 Oct 18

2 Retweets 4 Likes

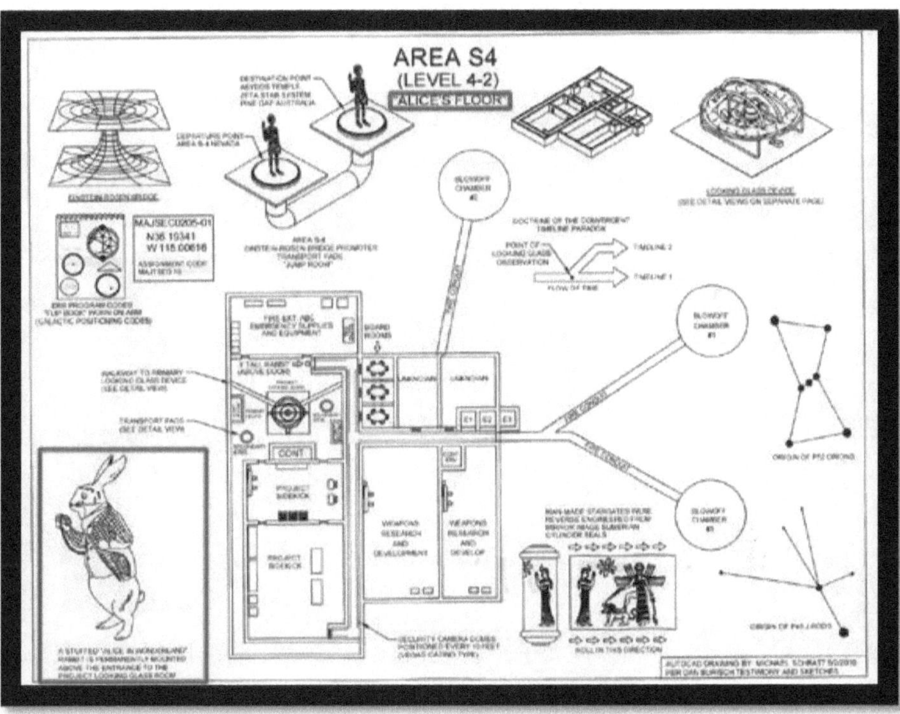
AREA S4
(LEVEL 4-2)
"ALICE'S FLOOR"
EINSTEIN-ROSEN BRIDGE
MAJSEC D2205-01
N36.19341
W 115.00616
LOOKING GLASS DEVICE
(SEE DETAIL VIEWS ON SEPARATE PAGE)
BLOWOFF CHAMBER
DOCTRINE OF THE DOWNRIGHT TIMELINE PARADOX
TIMELINE 2
TIMELINE 1
FLOW OF TIME
ORIGIN OF P52 ORIONS
ROLL IN THIS DIRECTION
ORIGIN OF P40 LACIDS
AUTOCAD DRAWING BY: MICHAEL SCHRATT 5/2/2010
PER DAN BURISCH TESTIMONY AND SKETCHES.

Project Looking Glass

The Eyes
The Distraction
Blocked View
The Handoff
Inside pew

1961
2019

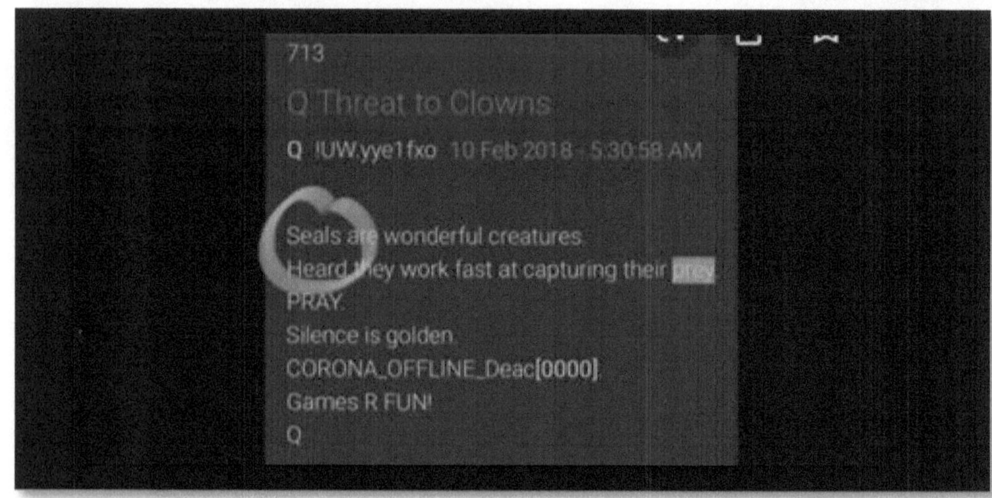
713

Q Threat to Clowns

Q !UW.yye1fxo 10 Feb 2018 - 5:30:58 AM

Seals are wonderful creatures.
Heard they work fast at capturing their prey.
PRAY.
Silence is golden.
CORONA_OFFLINE_Deac[0000].
Games R FUN!
Q

"...JFK's plane was sabotaged so it would crash." The motive? To eliminate the one political opponent that Hillary wouldn't have a prayer of beating in an election—the charming JFK Jr.
After the Senate, 'the next step would have been the White House'

FOX NATION
THE BIG STORY
THE DISAPPEARANCE OF JFK JR.
COMING MAY 16TH

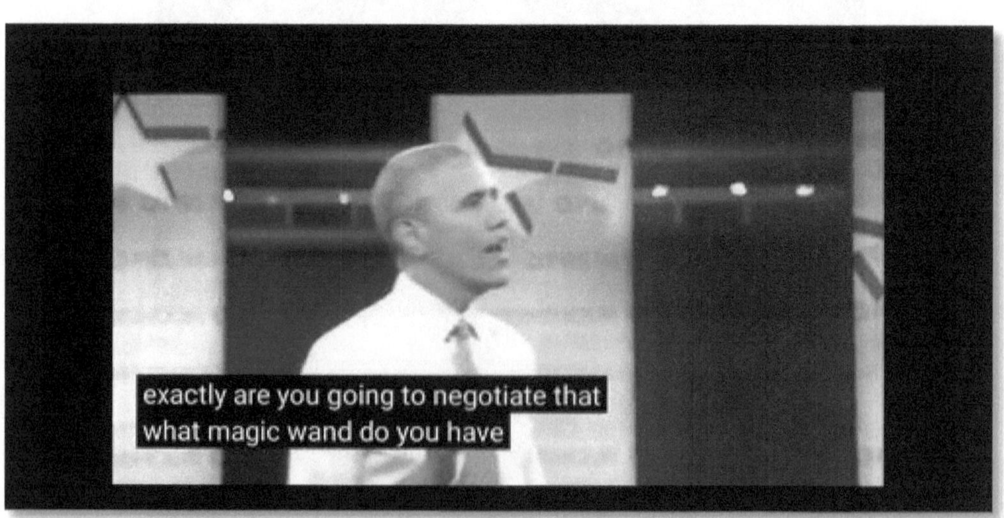
exactly are you going to negotiate that
what magic wand do you have

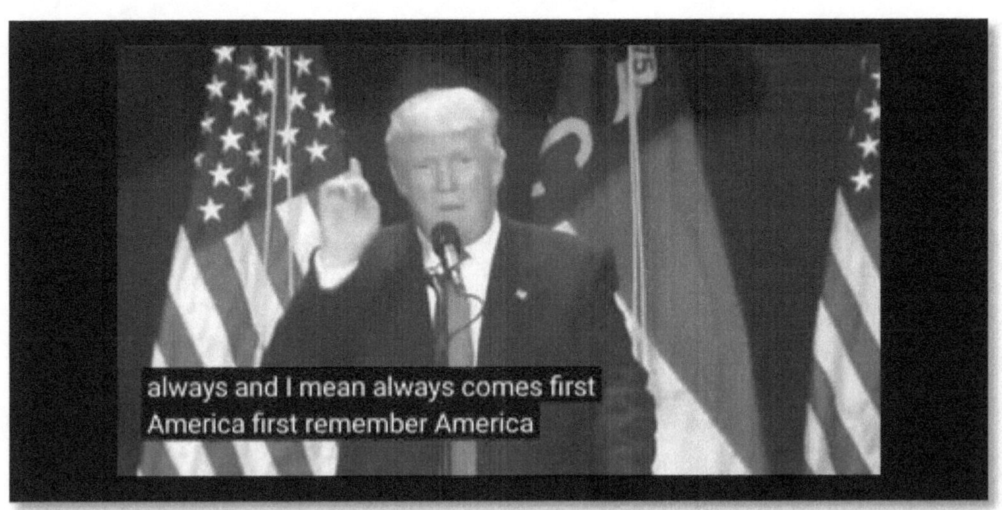
always and I mean always comes first
America first remember America

America first remember America first
America first

FEDERALIST SOCIETY
FedSo
ALIST
FedSo
FedSo
Fr
BREAKING NEWS
VP PENCE DIVERTED TO WASHINGTON MINUTES BEFORE
MANCHESTER ARRIVAL; WH: NOT AN EMERGENCY
WMUR
WMUR

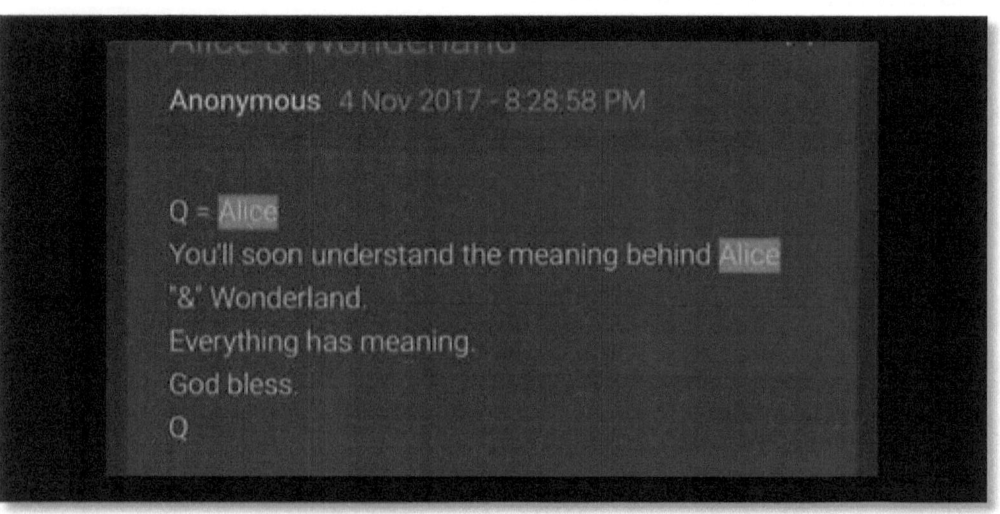

Alice & Wonderland
Anonymous   4 Nov 2017 - 8:28:58 PM
Q = Alice
You'll soon understand the meaning behind Alice
"&" Wonderland.
Everything has meaning.
God bless.
Q

 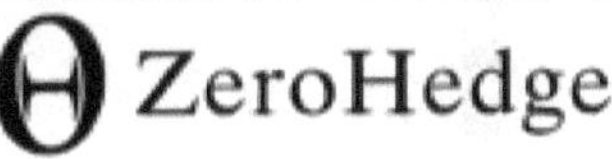

Michigan Passes Controversial Bill To Microchip Humans Voluntarily "To Protect Their Privacy"

by **Tyler Durden**
Sat, 07/04/2020 – 21:40

Via GreatGameIndia.com,

The Michigan House of Representatives has passed a controversial bill to microchip humans voluntarily in the state under the guise of protecting their privacy. The Microchip Protection Act would allow Michigan employers to use microchipping of their workers with their consent. However, research has shown that RFID transponders causes cancer.

3:09

Search Twitter

Log in
Sign up

John B Wells 11:11
@JohnBWellsCTM

BREAKING:

The #WorldHealthOrganization made a complete U turn and said that #coronavirus patients doesn't need to be isolated or quarantined. No #SocialDistancing and it cannot even transmit from one patient to another. *See the video.*
#coronascam

2:06 | 1.1M views
ASYMPTOMATIC CASES NOT INFECTIOUS

6:56 AM · Jul 3, 2020 · Twitter for Android

28.3K Retweets   24.9K Likes

Two Women Activists Hit by Car on I-5 Outside Seattle – Suffer Serious Injuries After Hitting Windshield and Front Grill .....Video

By Jim Hoft
Published July 4, 2020 at 10:36am

f Share (1.3k)

Study finds hydroxychloroquine helped coronavirus patients survive better

By Maggie Fox, Andrea Kane, an... 2 days ago

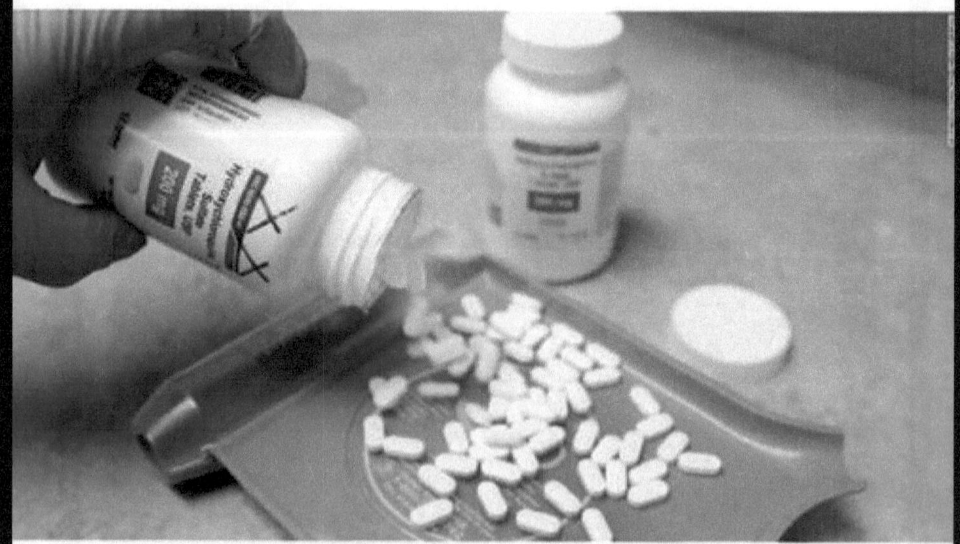

© **GEORGE FREY/AFP/AFP via Getty Images**
A pharmacy tech pours out pills of hydroxychloroquine at Rock Canyon Pharmacy in Provo, Utah, (Photo by GEORGE FREY / AFP) (Photo by GEORGE FREY/AFP via Getty Images)

BREAKING FROM ST. LOUIS: McCloskeys Have Armed Security Team on Balcony as BLM and Antifa Threaten Home on Friday Night

By Jim Hoft
Published July 3, 2020 at 7:52pm

Last weekend hundreds of Black Lives Matter and Antifa protesters broke through the gate on Portland Place, a private street in St. Louis.

Mark and Patricia McCloskey were eating dinner when the criminal mob marched down their street, painted the street and protested in front of Mayor Lyda Krewson's home.

BREAKING: White Couple Charged with Assault After Viral Video Shows Pregnant Woman Defending Herself with Firearm in Confrontation with Black Woman

By Cristina Laila
Published July 2, 2020 at 6:59pm

NEW YORK POST

Lawyer for Epstein victims thinks Ghislaine Maxwell will die in jail

Ghislaine Maxwell 'groomed' young assistant for Jeffrey Epstein, suit claims

Texas quadripleg COVID-19 after ho refuses treatmen claims

NEWS

Investigators eye Guinness beer aristocrat amid Ghislaine Maxwell's arrest

By Natalie Musumeci

July 3, 2020 | 3:10pm

James Woods ✔ @RealJamesWo… · 51m

You don't care about this person or these issues or anything but your own ruthless ambition. Get back on your knees where you started your career and shut up. #Hypocrite #HeelsUpHarris

Kamala Harris ✔ @KamalaHarr… · 10h

Absolutely heartbreaking. Summer Taylor was only 24-years-old, peacefully protesting for Black Lives Matter when they were struck by a car. Thinking of their family during this difficult time and every…

Nuke Pro

Exposing Truth - Sign up as a Follower

Climate, Earthquake, and Vulcanism Resources ▼

WEDNESDAY, NOVEMBER 27, 2019

Epstein Temple Modeled After "The Mamluks" Which Are White Slaves Forced to Convert to Islam

stock here

"Civil Disobedience"

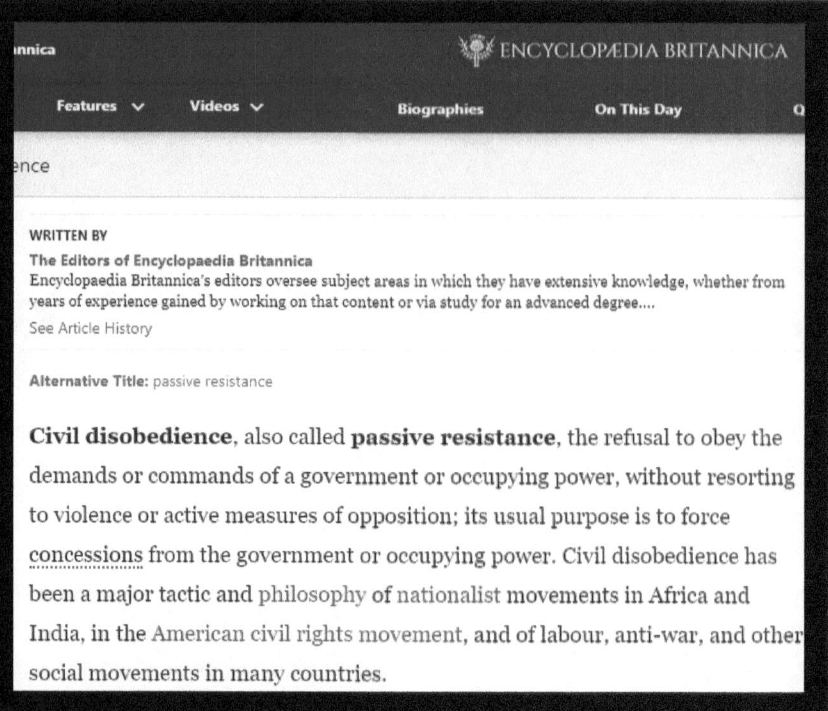

WRITTEN BY

The Editors of Encyclopaedia Britannica
Encyclopaedia Britannica's editors oversee subject areas in which they have extensive knowledge, whether from years of experience gained by working on that content or via study for an advanced degree....
See Article History

Alternative Title: passive resistance

Civil disobedience, also called **passive resistance**, the refusal to obey the demands or commands of a government or occupying power, without resorting to violence or active measures of opposition; its usual purpose is to force concessions from the government or occupying power. Civil disobedience has been a major tactic and philosophy of nationalist movements in Africa and India, in the American civil rights movement, and of labour, anti-war, and other social movements in many countries.

CNN politics   Donald Trump   Supreme Court   Congress   Facts First   2020 Election   + LIVE TV   Edition ∨

Michigan closes state Capitol as protesters gather against stay-at-home order

By Veronica Stracqualursi, CNN
Updated 7:21 PM ET, Thu May 14, 2020

Whitmer: Stay-at-home protests look like political rally 03:24

(CNN) — The Michigan state Capitol was closed Thursday as demonstrators gathered at the steps of the building to protest Gov. Gretchen Whitmer's stay-at-home order.

The latest protest and the Capitol's closure came two weeks after protesters, some armed, entered the building and demanded to be allowed into the legislative chambers, which have been closed due to social distancing measures. Photos from the day showed some protesters, many of whom were not wearing masks or standing more than 6 feet from one another,

<u>Democrat Insanity</u>

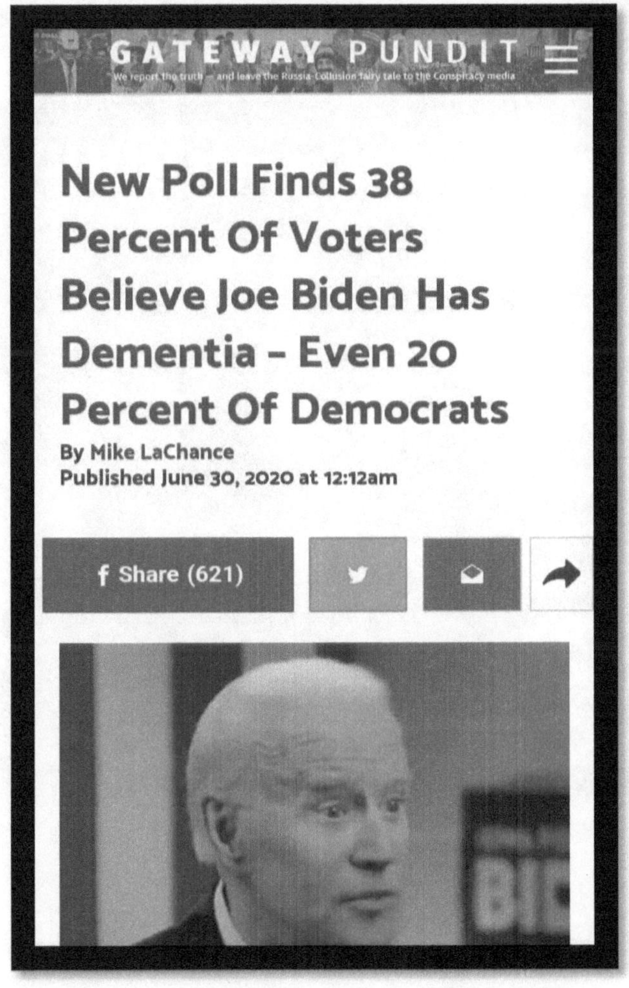

Will everyone who voted for the 1994 Crime Bill please take a knee

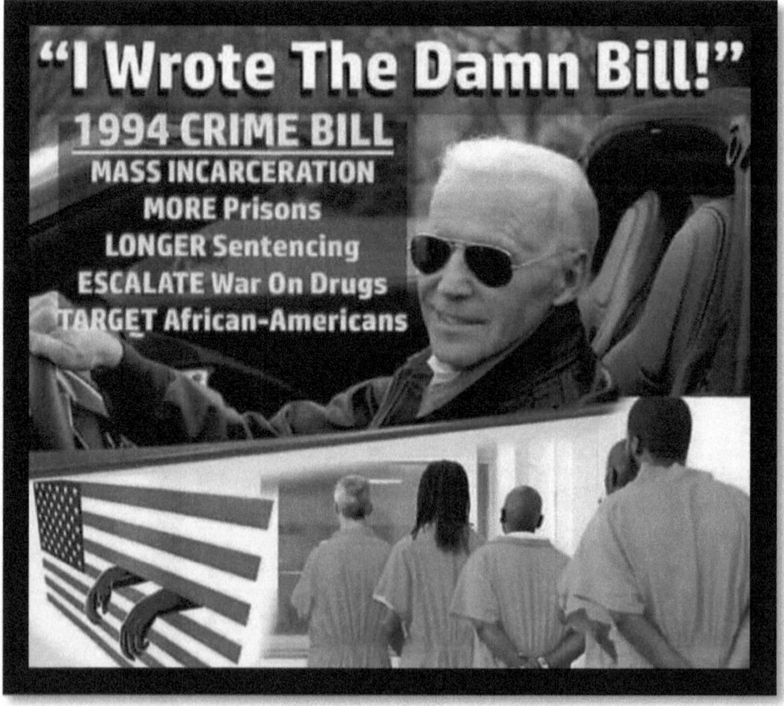
"I Wrote The Damn Bill!"
1994 CRIME BILL
MASS INCARCERATION
MORE Prisons
LONGER Sentencing
ESCALATE War On Drugs
TARGET African-Americans

Whos old enough to remember when we had:
- A Black President.
- A Black AG (2 of them!)
- A Democrat-Controlled House AND Senate.
- A VP who claims he's always worked for the Black community.

YET, they passed NO prison reform, NO police reform, or any other reforms for that matter!

(Stop the spread of stupidity and insanity!)

NYT TARGETS MOUNT RUSHMORE: INDIGENOUS LAND, KKK TIES, SLAVE OWNER PRESIDENTS

by HANNAH BLEAU | 1 Jul 2020

LISTEN TO STORY   4:47

The *New York Times* has set its sights on Mount Rushmore as protesters demand the removal of historic monuments in the name of racial justice, citing its location on "Indigenous land," the sculptor's purported ties to white supremacy, and two of its subjects' slave ownership.

"Mount Rushmore was built on land that belonged to the Lakota tribe and sculpted by a man who had strong bonds with the Ku Klux Klan. It features the faces of 2 U.S. presidents who were slaveholders," the *New York Times* wrote, linking to a news article detailing complaints against American landmark:

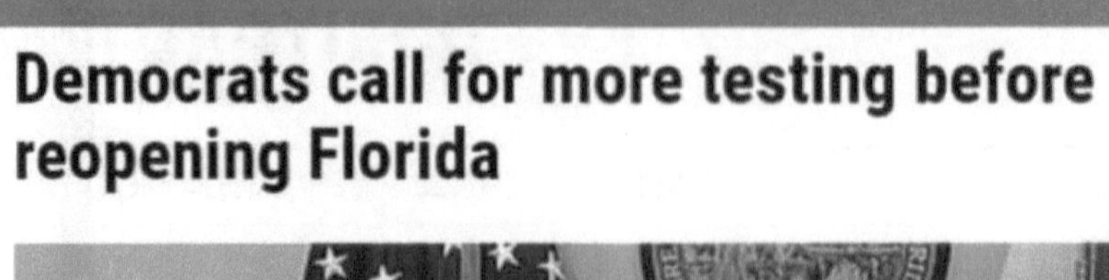

Democrats call for more testing before reopening Florida

by: Jake Stofan

Posted: Apr 20, 2020 / 03:51 PM EDT / Updated: Apr 20, 2020 / 03:51 PM EDT

CNN
"MOSTLY
PEACEFUL PROTEST"
REMOVE THE WHITMER REGIME
LIVE FREE OR DIE
END THE LOCKDOWN
CNN
imgflip.com
"DOMESTIC TERRORISTS"

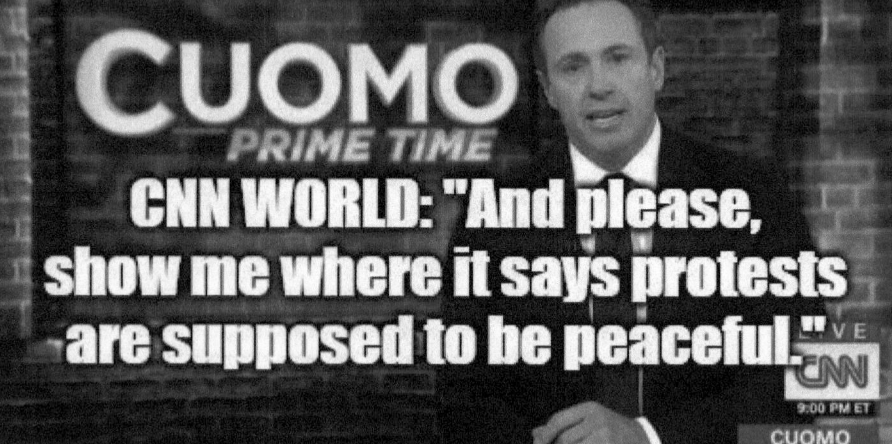

The First Amendment:

Congress shall make no law respecting an establishment of religion, or prohibiting the free exercise thereof; or abridging the freedom of speech, or of the press; or the right of the people peaceably to assemble, and to petition the Government for a redress of

UMM...THE CONSTITUTION?

Democrats are grappling with calls to "defund the police"

POLITICS / 2020 PROTESTS

Top Democrats Are Refusing To "Defund The Police." Activists Fear The Police Killings Won't Stop.

Reform leaders are frustrated with Democrats who have pushed aside the "defund the polic call that's central to protests against police brutality after George Floyd's killing.

Posted on June 18, 2020, at 1:50 p.m. ET

(Related: Feminist insanity)

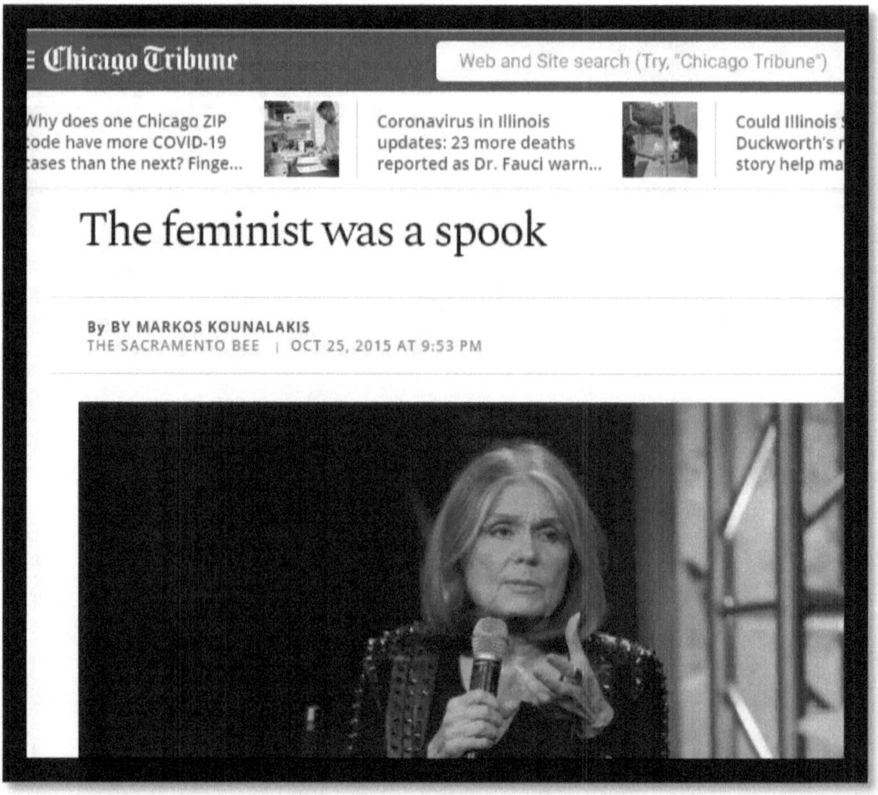

Relationships

Many Women Are Happier Single

by Sa'iyda Shabazz

December 18, 2017 | Updated December 13, 2019

Being a single woman can be a real challenge. We're constantly asked "So, are you dating anyone?" And if we say no, it's usually followed up with "Well, why not?" Many people, especially those who are in relationships, or those who enjoy dating, just don't understand.

But a recent **poll** found that 61% of women say they're happy being single, compared to 49% of happily single men. Although the poll comes out of the UK, but I'd wager to guess that it's fairly similar in America. The report, published by company Mintel, also states that of those 61% of women, 75% of them haven't pursued a relationship in the past year. And I think I know why.

Dating for women is exhausting! In this swipe left/swipe right culture, women have to jump through hoops to get a second glance. We need to have the total package just based on our pictures. There are more expectations placed on women, than men, when it comes to dating. Dating is a hustle that turns into a grind, and I'm not talking about dancing or a great night in bed.

Women have to look amazing, act amazing, be amazing. And men can do the bare minimum and always find a date. Frankly, it's bullshit.

If women are being held to unrealistic standards when it comes to dating, it's easier to stay single. That way, we can put our energy into the kinds of things *we want* to be putting our energy into.

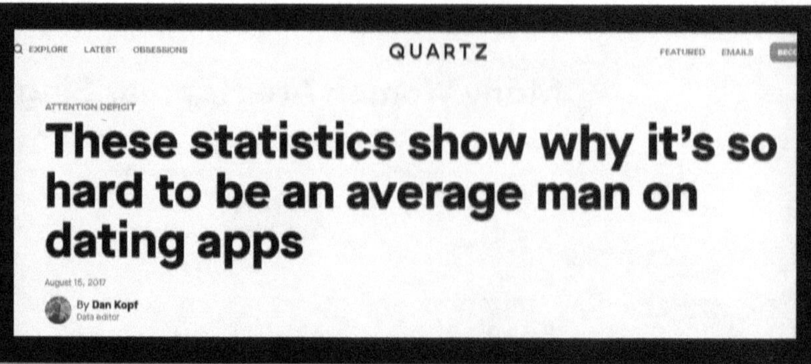

These statistics show why it's so hard to be an average man on dating apps

August 15, 2017

By **Dan Kopf**
Data editor

QUARTZ

Dating apps are tough on the middle-of-the-road guy. If you are not one of the most desirable men on the app, you probably are not getting much attention.

Aviv Goldgeier, an engineer for the dating website Hinge, recently analyzed the share of "likes" on Hinge that went to the most-liked people of each gender. He found that inequality on dating apps is stark, and that it was significantly worse for men. The top 1% of guys get more than 16% of all likes on the app, compared to just over 11% for the top 1% of women. (Unlike swipe-based Tinder, Hinge is based on a system of "liking" some particular aspect of a person's profile.)

Group	Men	Women
Top 1%	16.4%	11.2%
Top 5%	41.1%	30.6%
Top 10%	58.0%	45.7%
Bottom 50%	4.3%	7.9%

The reason for this gender disparity is probably not that women are more appearance-focused than men. The most likely explanation is that women, who are generally less likely to initiate contact, have a higher threshold when they do so. For many women, though certainly not all, if they are going to break with gender norms, it is only going to be for a really attractive guy.

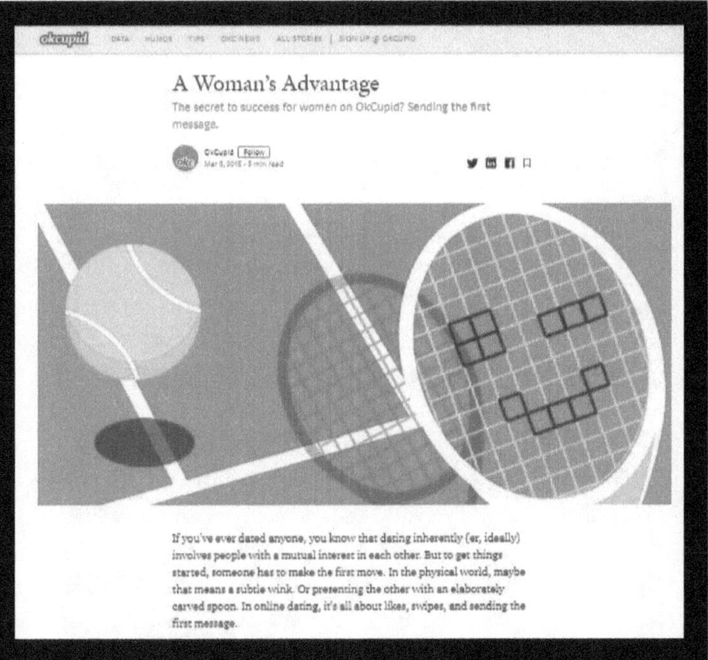

A Woman's Advantage

The secret to success for women on OkCupid? Sending the first message.

If you've ever dated anyone, you know that dating inherently (er, ideally) involves people with a mutual interest in each other. But to get things started, someone has to make the first move. In the physical world, maybe that means a subtle wink. Or presenting the other with an elaborately carved spoon. In online dating, it's all about likes, swipes, and sending the first message.

The OkCupid Blog
Reflections on dating culture, told through data, stories...

Follow

66

Traditionally, men take the initiative. At least that's what we can discern from most examples of romance in Western culture. On OkCupid however, women and men exhibit similar behavior when it comes to liking, browsing and having conversations. The playing field is also pretty even: there are 1.5 men for every woman on the site. These women are progressive too, with 43 percent of women preferring to split the check (compared to 17 percent of men).

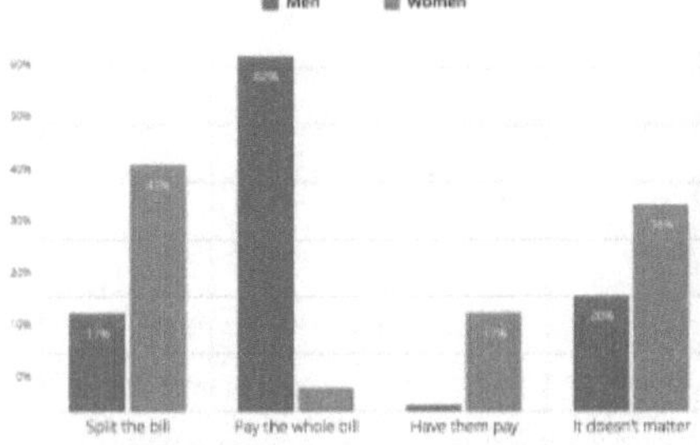

Yet there is one crucial way in which women fail to take the lead. Most women — regardless of sexual orientation — do not send the first message, with straight woman 3.5x less likely to compared to straight men.

(Astonishing that people can actually get paid for writing this stuff - "Feminists" appear to have a very low standard for logic, reason, or even common decency and a basic standard of ethical morality — The ultimate sociopathic narcissists)

Sex is the very least of our concerns, the last thing that has to be crossed off the to-do list. Or so I have heard from harassed women in the school playground. Yet sex is the very meaning of life, the cement that glues together every relationship, half our culture also tells us, while the remainder portrays women as a series of orifices to be penetrated.

Perhaps sex is all and none of these things. When people write to experts asking for help, their problems inevitably boil down to: "I want more or less sex, or of a different kind, or with a different person from the one I am currently having sex with."

This is why the idea of women going on sex strike as a form of resistance is a no-go, although the latest person to suggest one, the actor Alyssa Milano, is right to be appalled by Georgia's "heartbeat law", which means a woman could be imprisoned for having an abortion after six weeks of pregnancy. We all get where Milano is coming from - or not coming from - for sex is attention-grabbing.

Inevitably, much whataboutery has followed this oldest of ideas: what about lesbians, sex workers, trans people or women who actually want sex?

What does the withholding of sex do? I always think of Mrs Merton on the three words every man wants to hear: "If you must." If withholding is a political action, then the go-slow of many long-term relationships - the pressing of the shared snooze button - is, er, radical.

What I really like about this is the strike bit, not the sex bit. If we women

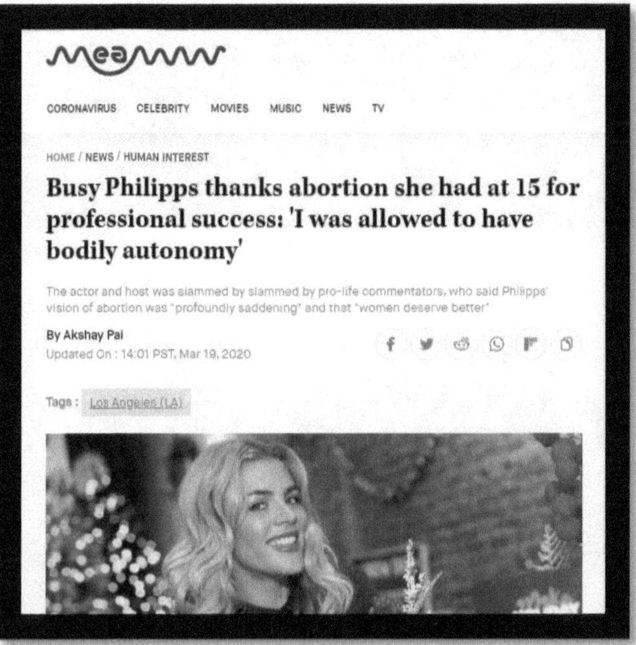

(Poor misled little girl)

the
FEDERALIST
A DIVISION OF FDRLST MEDIA

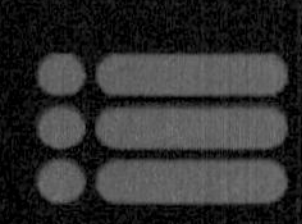

ABORTION

Under Sworn Testimony, Planned Parenthood Officials Admit Infanticide Occurs In Organ Harvesting

JUNE 30, 2020 By Madeline Osburn

Lila Rose ✔
@LilaGraceRose

BREAKING:

Multiple Planned Parenthood officials have admitted under oath to trafficking the body parts & organs of babies they slaughtered.

These are criminal acts.

@TheJusticeDept, #ShutThemDown

5:50 PM · May 26, 2020 · Twitter Web App

4324

Bombshell: Planned Parenthood Officials Admit under Oath to Selling Aborted Body Parts

Q !!Hs1Jq13jV6 26 May 2020 - 8:26:08 PM

https://twitter.com/LilaGraceRose/status/1265430130274385922

These people are sick!

Q

"Kung-Flu" Hoax

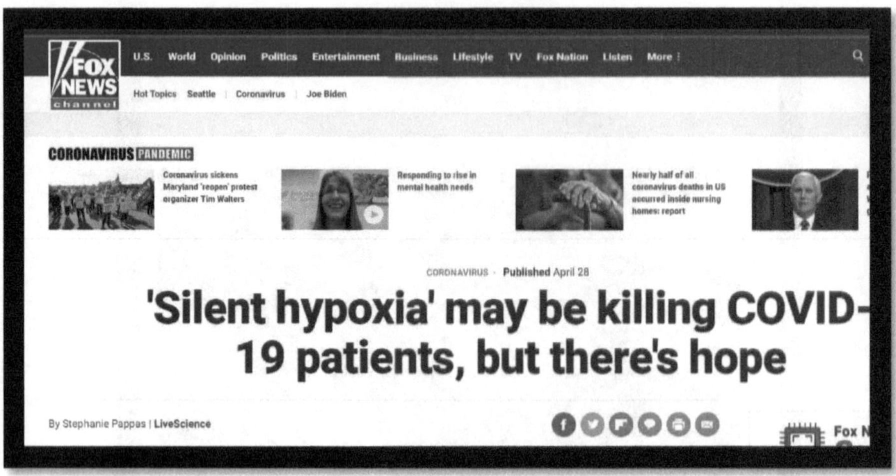

"Hypoxia" is the starvation of your body of oxygen - People who supposedly die of the mythical "Coronavirus" die from "Hypoxia" - Wearing a mask reduces oxygen intake and leads to Hypoxia - They are trying to drive up the number of "Hypoxia" deaths in order to drive up the "Coronavirus" deaths, get it?

All that is required to determine "Coronavirus" as a "cause of death" is matching the symptoms without a test, or even if someone is asymptomatic but had a house member diagnosed with "Coronavirus"... And then the hospital gets awarded about $15,000 by the government for a "Coronavirus"-related death - Why is the government providing a financial incentive to lie and kill people?

Nursing homes? Who are they killing? A significant percentage of the Republican voter base, older Americans, that's who - This is war, and the "mask" is a weapon being enforced against us.

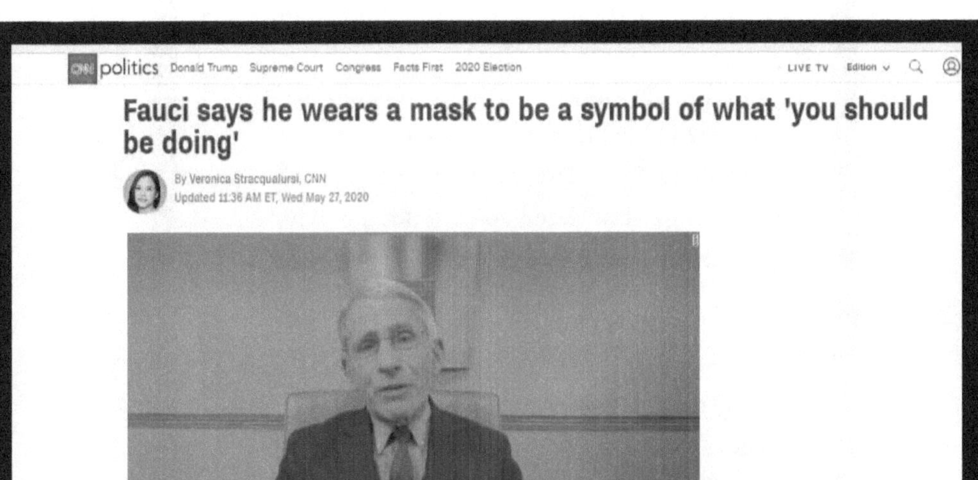

CNN politics   Donald Trump   Supreme Court   Congress   Facts First   2020 Election   LIVE TV   Edition
Fauci says he wears a mask to be a symbol of what 'you should be doing'
By Veronica Stracqualursi, CNN
Updated 11:36 AM ET, Wed May 27, 2020

NEWS   AFTER GEORGE FLOYD   CORONAVIRUS   POLITICS   OPINION   U.S. NEWS   BUSINESS   WORLD   PRIDE 2020   PODCASTS
Do you need a mask? The science hasn't changed, but public guidance might
Attitudes about masks are beginning to change in the US, both among the general public and at the highest levels of public health.
A woman covers her face as she crosses through Times Square in New York on March 22.
By Erika Edwards
As coronavirus cases continue to rise, a growing number of Americans are opting to cover their noses and mouths with makeshift masks, including bandannas, scarves or other wraps, when venturing into public.

USA TODAY NEWS

•**Masks.** The only people who need masks are those who are already infected to keep from exposing others. The masks sold at drugstores aren't even good enough to truly protect anyone, Fauci said.

"If you look at the masks that you buy in a drug store, the leakage around that doesn't really do much to protect you," he said. "People start saying, 'Should I start wearing a mask?' Now, in the United States, there is absolutely no reason whatsoever to wear a mask."

MARCH 2020: DR. ANTHONY FAUCI TALKS WITH DR JON LAPOOK ABOUT COVID-19

In March, Fauci told 60 Minutes that masks should largely be reserved for healthcare providers. In April, the recommendations were broadened to include simple masks for the general public.

2020
MAR 08

BY
BRIT MCCANDLESS FARMER

FACEBOOK
TWITTER
REDDIT
FLIPBOARD

Forbes   Billionaires   Innovation   Leadership   Money   Business   Small Business   Lifestyle   Li

BREAKING | 61,963 views | Mar 31, 2020, 03:08pm EDT

Should Americans Wear Masks Outside The House? Dr. Anthony Fauci Now Says Maybe

Marley Coyne Former Staff
Business
I cover breaking news.

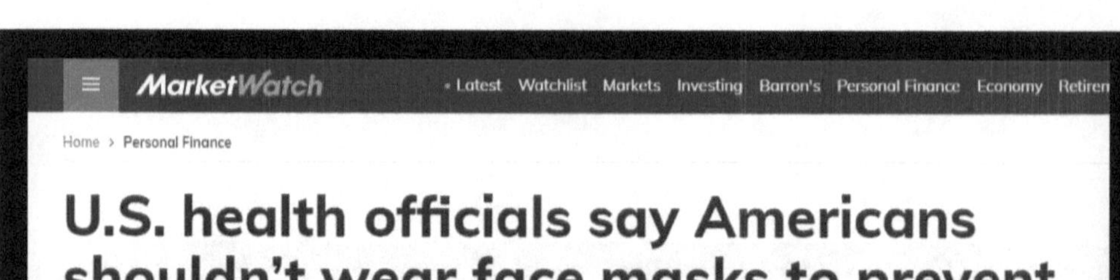

U.S. health officials say Americans shouldn't wear face masks to prevent coronavirus — here are 3 other reasons not to wear them

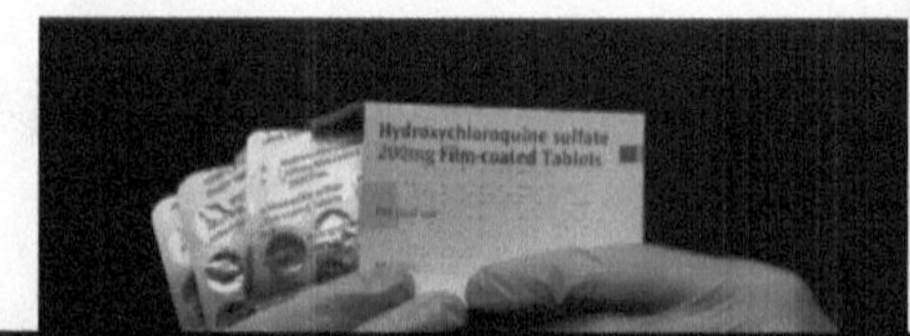

POLITICO

HEALTH CARE

FDA ends emergency use of hydroxychloroquine for coronavirus

The agency now believes that the suggested dosing regimens "are unlikely to produce an antiviral effect," FDA chief scientist Denise Hinton said in a letter.

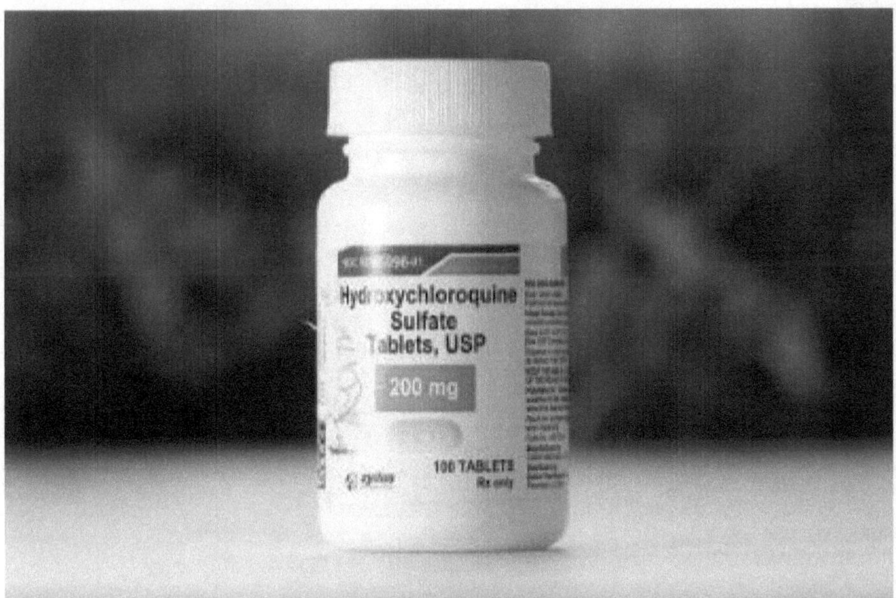

A bottle of hydroxychloroquine tablets. | David J. Phillip, File/AP Photo

By SARAH OWERMOHLE
06/15/2020 11:20 AM EDT
Updated: 06/15/2020 11:52 AM EDT

Newsmax

Independent. American.

Search Newsmax

Latest BLITZ Author Tells Glenn Beck: Trump Most 'Slandered Man' in History

Home | America

Tags: Coronavirus | Coronavirus Special | Health Topics | Cold/Flu | who | transmission | asymptomatic

WHO: Asymptomatic Virus Transmission 'Very Rare'

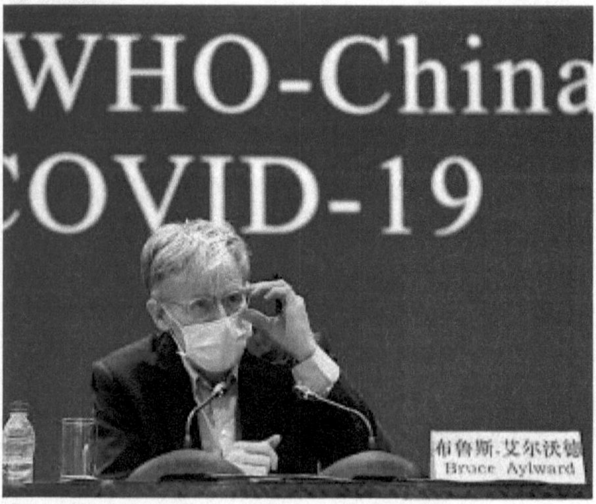

(AP)

By Marisa Herman | Monday, 08 June 2020 05:31 PM

Share Like

Short URL | Email Article | Comments | Contact | Print | A A

The World Health Organization said Monday the spread of coronavirus from asymptomatic patients is "very rare."

Fake Racism, "Reverse Racism" *is* "Racism,"

& Racism Does Not Exist

"...all ***TEN*** unarmed blacks killed by police last year."

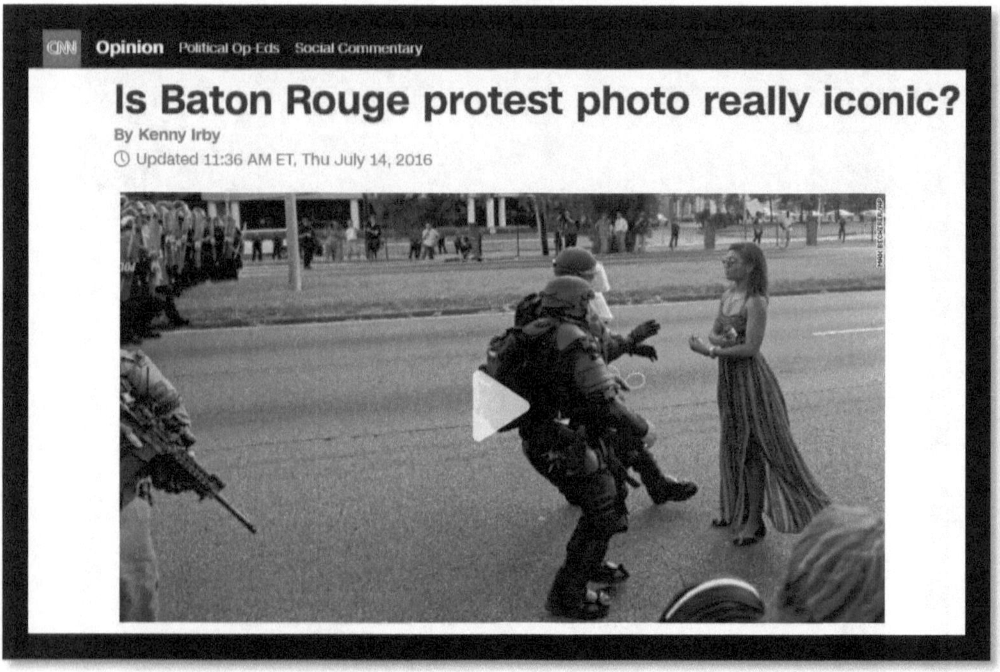
CNN
Opinion
Political Op-Eds
Social Commentary
Is Baton Rouge protest photo really iconic?
By Kenny Irby
Updated 11:36 AM ET, Thu July 14, 2016

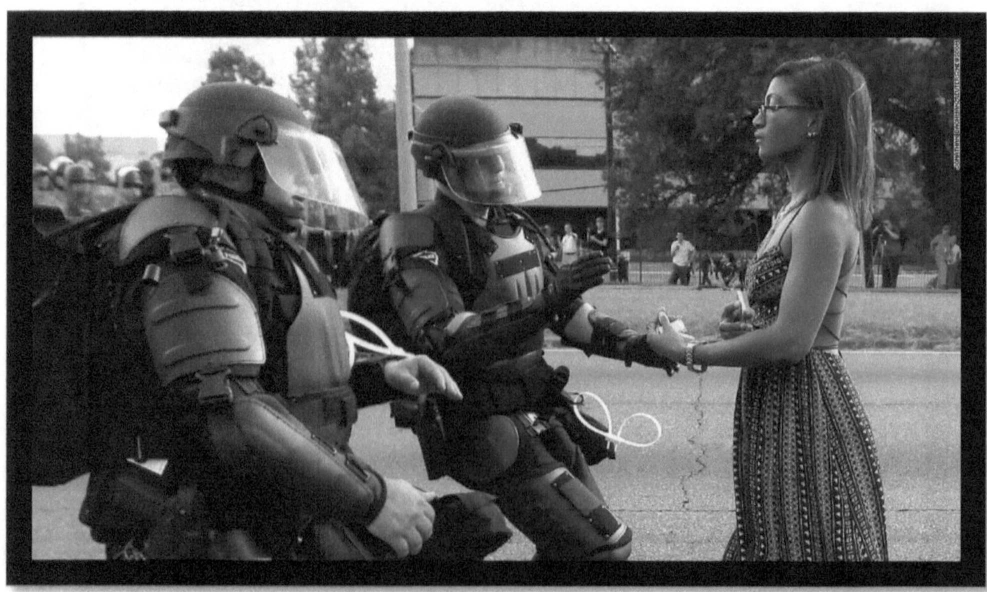

The story behind this viral photo 01:58

Story highlights

Kenny Irby: Iconic photos are rare, carry weight of an entire story, transport viewer; is Baton Rouge photo iconic?

Irby: Photo of protesting woman is image of grace under pressure, memorably arresting, but it's too early to label iconic

Editor's Note: Kenny Irby recently joined the St. Petersburg Police Department as its community intervention director. He is a former photojournalist, picture editor and educator. He founded Poynter's internationally accredited photojournalism program and was a 20-year senior faculty member until October 2015. The opinions expressed in this commentary are solely those of the author.

(CNN) — Attack dogs unleashed in Birmingham, Alabama, in 1963; the Tiananmen Square tank standoff in 1989; an Egyptian protester in a blue bra being beaten in Cairo in 2011 — all iconic images now associated with historical moments in time.

But what makes an image iconic?

The true iconic image is rare and unlike any other. It is the sum total of many elements, vetted against cultural, professional and historic standards.

Kenny Irby

It carries the weight of an entire story, even movement, in one photograph. It transports. Audiences instantly share it and reporters tell stories using it as a critical visual backdrop.

Right now, across social media and embedded in mainstream media coverage, people are discussing a powerful, decisive moment documented by Jonathan Bachman of Reuters.

(Mr. Irby… as affable and deadly as most run-of-the-mill modern communist propaganda artists)

On a humid Sunday afternoon in July, Bachman captured Ieshia Evans, 35, in a flowing gray spotted summer dress (what members of the African-American community might call her "Sunday's best"), defiantly standing her ground during a Baton Rouge protest against police officers in riot gear.

She had joined dozens of protesters along Baton Rouge's Airline Highway to denounce the death four days earlier of Alton Sterling, shot by police outside a local convenience store. Many protesters carried signs. A few shouted into bullhorns. And some were reported to have armed themselves with guns.

Related Article: How Giuliani misreads Black Lives Matter

Later arrested, Evans joined a long list of American citizens apprehended for exercising her right to participate in civil disobedience, to stand for justice denied.

Follow @CNNOpinion

Like so many photographs quickly tagged by the media as "iconic," this image has inspired a flurry of articles, commentary and online discourse.

Is it iconic?

Evans can certainly be seen to represent a certain peace amid a storm of protest against injustice, a storm that is rippling as a wave across our not so United States of America.

In the era of #BlackLivesMatter, she is a maiden of grace, reminiscent of a Statue of Liberty-like figure, unflappably standing her ground before an animated flurry of armed-to-the-teeth police officers, protesters and bystanders.

In a fraction of a second she embodied a special quality of guts and courage: "grace under pressure," is how Ernest Hemingway defined it.

Join us on Facebook.com/CNNOpinion.

Some see in this photographic image a reminder of other photographs indelibly etched in their photographic memories. The contrast recalls images of the stand-off between a man and a tank in Tiananmen Square in 1989, or the determination of Rosa Parks in refusing to give up her seat on a segregated city bus in 1955.

Related Article: Black skin: A uniform we can't take off

For me, Bachman's image bears an eerie resemblance to one made by Oded Balilty of the Associated Press. It won the 2007 Pulitzer Prize for breaking news photography, and showed a lone Jewish woman defying heavily armed Israeli security forces as they attempted to demolish the homes of illegal settlers in the West Bank.

Bachman told Buzzfeed that his photo "was the first image I transferred [to Reuters] because I knew it was going to be an important photo ... you can take images of plenty of people getting arrested, but I think this one speaks more to the movement and what the demonstrators are trying to accomplish here in Baton Rouge."

Truth be told, it's too early to label Bachman's photograph iconic. It has yet to be measured against a broader body of photographic works, juried in the photojournalism world of contests, or evaluated by historians and pundits in academic halls.

But without question, this image of grace under pressure is memorably arresting.

(Wow… I imagine that Mr. Irby scored really good grades in English literature classes at whatever overpriced university he attended)

BET co-founder Robert Johnson: 'Black people laugh at White people' who topple statues

'An attempt by White Americans to assuage guilt by doing things that make them feel good'

Black Entertainment Television co-founder and billionaire philanthropist Robert Johnson appeared on Fox News on Wednesday, June 24, 2020. (screengrab via Fox News) more ›

  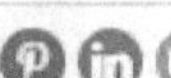  

🖨 Print

By Jessica Chasmar - The Washington Times - Thursday, June 25, 2020

Black Entertainment Television co-founder and billionaire philanthropist Robert Johnson said Wednesday that "Black people laugh at White people" who topple statues in the name of racial justice.

During an appearance on Fox News, Mr. Johnson ripped the vandals who are defacing and tearing down statues of the Founding Fathers and Confederate generals across the country as a protest against systemic racism in the wake of the police-custody death of George Floyd.

THE FIRST AFRICAN-AMERICAN TO RECEIVE THE
MEDAL OF HONOR IN THE CIVIL WAR WAS SGT.
WILLIAM HARVEY CARNEY WHO, DESPITE BEING
SHOT IN THE FACE, SHOULDERS, ARMS, AND
LEGS, REFUSED TO LET THE AMERICAN FLAG
TOUCH THE GROUND.

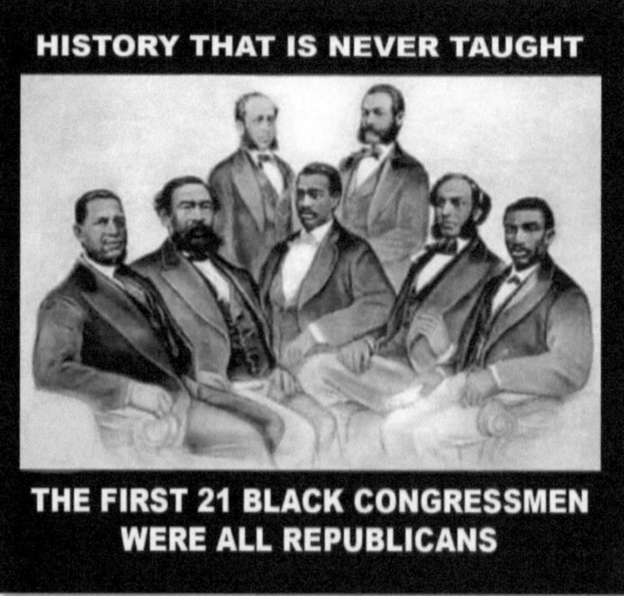
HISTORY THAT IS NEVER TAUGHT
THE FIRST 21 BLACK CONGRESSMEN
WERE ALL REPUBLICANS

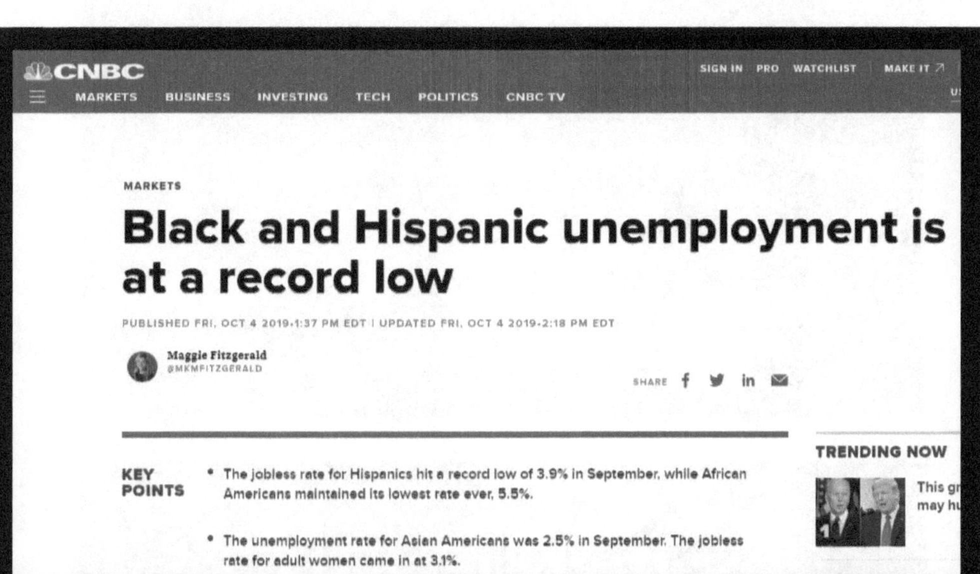

Black and Hispanic unemployment is at a record low

“INFORMATION WARFARE”

4499

INFORMATION WARFARE

Q !!Hs1Jq13jV6 22 Jun 2020 - 7:47:04 PM

INFORMATION WARFARE.

Q

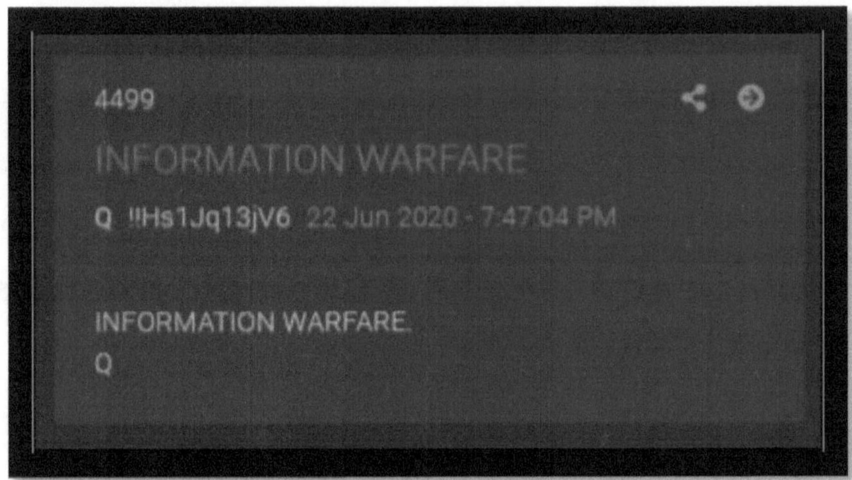

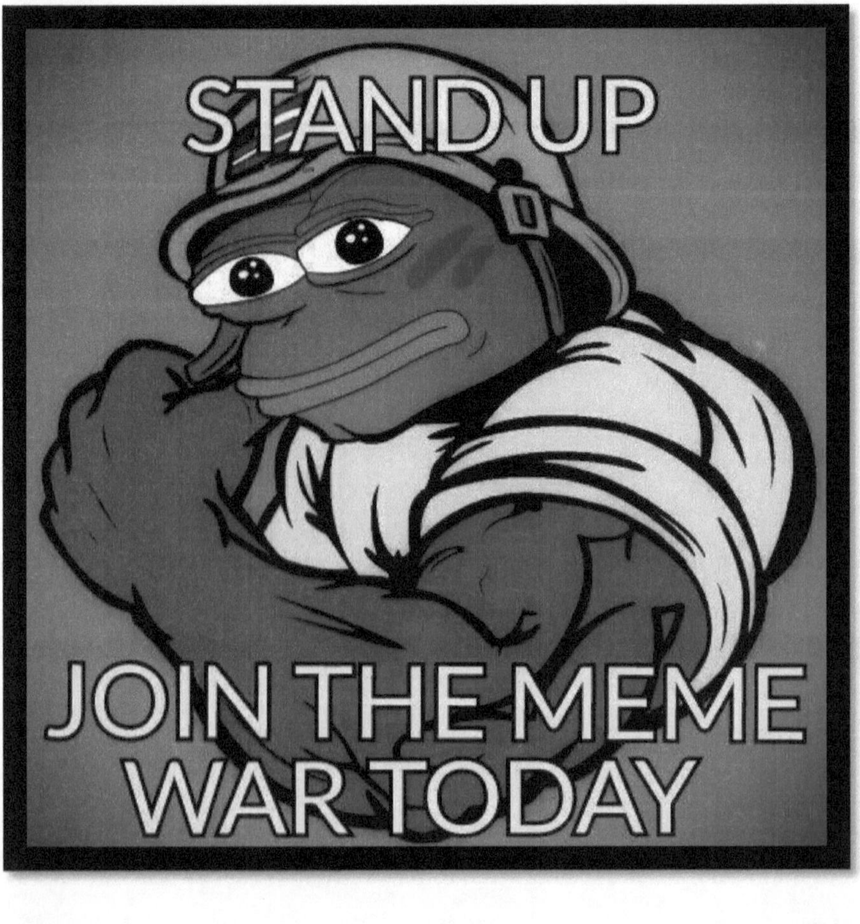

<u>"INFILTRATION V INVASION"</u>

4373

THE GREATEST [COORDINATED] DISINFORMATION CAMPAIGN TO EVER BE LAUNCHED AGAINST THE AMERICAN PEOPLE

Q !!Hs1Jq13jV6 31 May 2020 - 6:47:15 PM

YOU ARE WITNESSING THE GREATEST [COORDINATED] DISINFORMATION CAMPAIGN TO EVER BE LAUNCHED AGAINST THE AMERICAN PEOPLE.
INFORMATION WARFARE.
INFILTRATION V INVASION
INSURGENCY.
IRREGULAR WARFARE.
[D] EFFORTS TO REGAIN POWER.
Q

Huma Abedin's ties to the Muslim Brotherhood

BY KENNETH R. TIMMERMAN, CONTRIBUTOR · 08/23/16 11:29 AM EDT

13,117 SHARES

Just In...

Michelle Obama presents Beyoncé with Humanitarian Award at BET Awards: 'You inspire all of us'

The Clinton campaign is attempting once again to sweep important questions under the rug about top aide Huma Abedin, her family ties to the Muslim Brotherhood and to Saudi Arabia, and her role in the ballooning Clinton email scandal.

CONTRIBUTOR'S S
Sign up to become a C

4284

Huma Abedin's Ties to the Muslim Brotherhood

Q !!Hs1Jq13jV6 19 May 2020 - 11:04:06 AM

https://thehill.com/blogs/pundits-blog/presidential-campaign/292310-huma-abedins-ties-to-the-muslim-brotherhood

Infiltration not invasion.
For future events.
Q

M3thods
@M2Madness

Michele Bachmann called out the infiltration by the Muslim Brotherhood back in 2012...

7:36 PM · Feb 24, 2020 · Twitter Web App

4036

Michele Bachmann Called out the Infiltration by the Muslim Brotherhood Back in 2012

Q !!Hs1Jq13jV6 30 Apr 2020 - 8:54:10 PM

https://twitter.com/M2Madness/status/12321321713
44773121 

Q

RealClear Politics ⌄   Polls

← Back to Videos

Mark Levin: "The Muslim Brotherhood Has Infiltrated Our Government, It's Called Barack Obama"

Posted By Ian Schwartz
On Date January 31, 2013

4035

Mark Levin: The Muslim Brotherhood Has Infiltrated Our Government, It's Called Barack Obama

Q !!Hs1Jq13jV6 30 Apr 2020 - 8:50:48 PM

https://www.realclearpolitics.com/video/2013/01/31/
mark_levin_the_muslim_brotherhood_has_infiltrated_o
ur_government_its_called_barack_obama.html

Q

Tensions flare on Senate floor over GOP Senator's Muslim Brotherhood remarks

By CHEYNA ROTH · APR 26, 2018

 Share    Tweet    Email

Tensions were high on the Senate floor today, when a lawmaker doubled down on claims that Muslim terrorist groups are trying to infiltrate the U.S.

4034

Michigan Senator Calls Out Muslim Brotherhood's "Civialization Jihad" Plot Against America

Q !!Hs1Jq13jV6 30 Apr 2020 - 8:45:10 PM

https://www.michiganradio.org/post/tensions-flare-senate-floor-over-gop-senator-s-muslim-brotherhood-remarks

Q

2080

Traitor: John McCain Senator for ISIS
and Muslim Brotherhood

Q !!mG7VJxZNCI 4 Sep 2018 - 11:47:53 AM

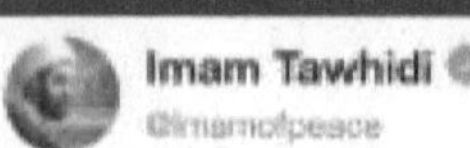

DmRHzKvXsAEfFMS.jpg

https://twitter.com/RealKyleMorris/status/1036782274203865088

https://twitter.com/imamofpeace/status/1036808475744002048

Q

John Kerry, Nancy Pelosi, Bashar Assad, Huma Abedin & Muslim Brotherhood Connection

Q !4pRcUA0lBE   13 May 2018 - 10:48:00 AM

7408979A-CC0C-4DA3-80A5-8...jpeg

13818358-8E2E-4659-A083-B...jpeg

Full Circle.

http://thehill.com/blogs/pundits-blog/presidential-campaign/292310-huma-abedins-ties-to-the-muslim-brotherhood

https://www.scribd.com/doc/100244266/Bachmann-Letter-Responding-to-Ellison

It's all connected.
Welcome back Huma.
Now comes the pain.
Q

1237

Muslim Brotherhood Plan to Destroy America

Q !xowAT4Z3VQ 21 Apr 2018 - 11:31:31 PM

"The process of settlement is a 'Civilization-Jihadist Process' with all the word means. The Ikhwan [**Muslim Brotherhood**] must understand that their work in America is a kind of grand jihad in eliminating and destroying the Western civilization from within and 'sabotaging' its miserable house by their hands and the hands of the believers..."

https://clarionproject.org/muslim_brotherhood_explanatory_memorandum/

Q

<u>White, Middle-Aged Males in The United States</u>

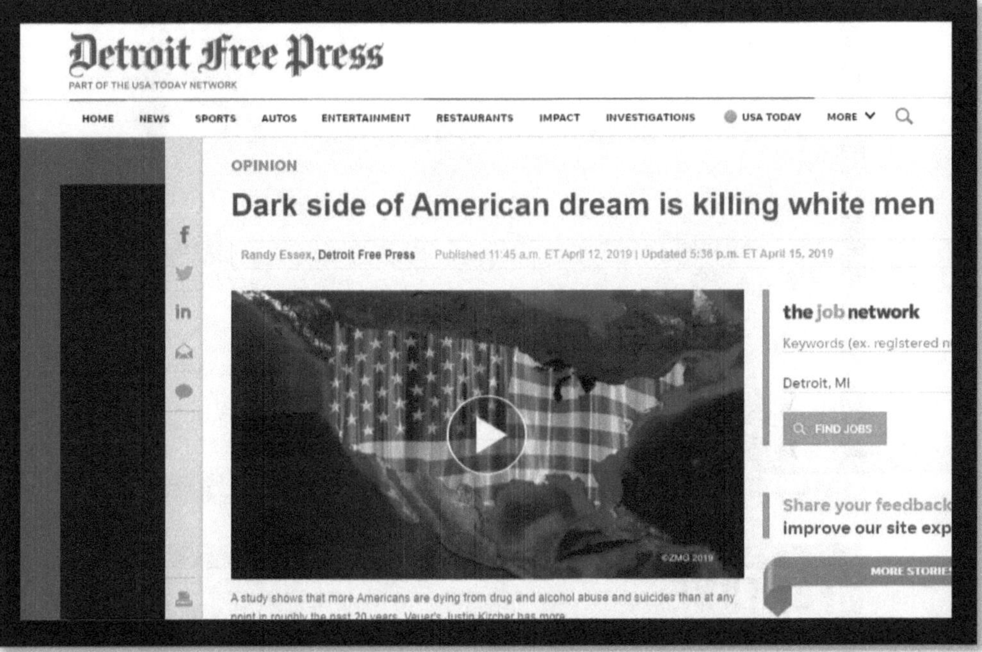

Donald Trump has a new target for his criticism of the nation's immigration policies - Facebook founder Mark Zuckerberg.

Zuckerberg is one of the leading tech executives who has called for a more open immigration policy. Specifically, he wants to make more H-1B visas available to tech employers so they can hire foreign skilled workers.

Trump said he wants to require employers to pay H-1B workers much more money, which he said would discourage companies from hiring them and boost job prospects for Americans. He also wants to have tech jobs offered to unemployed Americans before they can be filled by workers with H-1B visas.

"This will improve the number of black, Hispanic and female workers in Silicon Valley who have been passed over in favor of the H-1B program. Mark Zuckerberg's personal Senator, Marco Rubio, has a bill to triple H-1Bs that would decimate women and minorities," Trump wrote in his immigration plan. Rubio is also seeking the Republican nomination for president.

THE ECONOMIC TIMES | ITeS
LATEST NEWS Maharashtra extends
Home ▾ Tech Hardware Software Internet ITeS Tech and Gadgets
Business News › Tech › ITeS › US tech firms get more H-1B visas in FY19
Benchmarks ›
Nifty • CLOSED
10,312.40 ↓ -70.60
Stock Screener ›
Stocks with DII Buying
Stocks with FII Buying
Stocks with FII Selling
Search, Select & Invest in Top Stocks
FEATURED FUND
ICICI Prudential B
Fund Direct-Grow
★★★★
US tech firms get more H-1B visas in FY19
Seven US companies among top 10 recipients; TCS, Cognizant and TechM were others in the list. The top ten companies accounted for 12% of the 88324 H-1B visas issued in fiscal 2019.
By Ayan Pramanik, Priyanka Sangani, ET Bureau | Last Updated: Nov 05, 2019, 08 14 AM IST
Save
0 Comments
A+
Bengaluru | Pune: Seven US technology firms including Google, Amazon, Apple and Facebook were among the top ten recipients of fresh H-1B visas in fiscal year 2019, as the President Donald Trump administration continued its policy of favouring American firms to hire computer science professionals
H-1B

FORTUNE RANKINGS ⌄ MAGAZINE NEWSLETTERS VIDEO PODCASTS CONFERENCES COV
ENERGY
Fracking pioneer Chesapeake Energy files for bankruptcy
INTERNATIONAL
Swarms of locusts descend on India's biggest sugarcane region
RETAIL
Starbucks pauses all social media call for Facebook boycott
MPW · FORTUNE 500
The Fortune 500 Has More Female CEOs Than Ever Before
BY CLAIRE ZILLMAN
May 16, 2019 4.30 AM MDT

Q Search
Bloomberg Businessweek
December 12, 2019, 3:00 AM MST
Having More Women CEOs Won't Fix the Gender Gap
● Just putting more females in charge doesn't guarantee a healthy corporate culture.
By Rebecca Greenfield

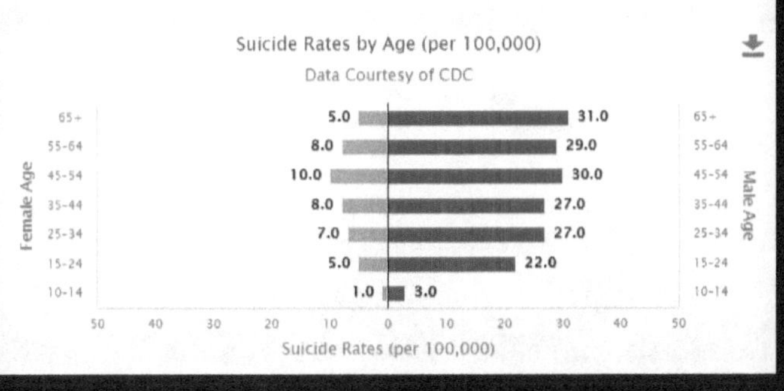

...hics

...uicide rates take population size into account, they can be a useful tool for understanding the relative proportion of people affected within different demographic groups.

- Figure 2 shows the crude rates of suicide within sex and age categories in 2017.
  - Among females, the suicide rate was highest for those aged 45-54 (10.0 per 100,000).
  - Among males, the suicide rate was highest for those aged 65 and older (31.0 per 100,000).

Figure 2

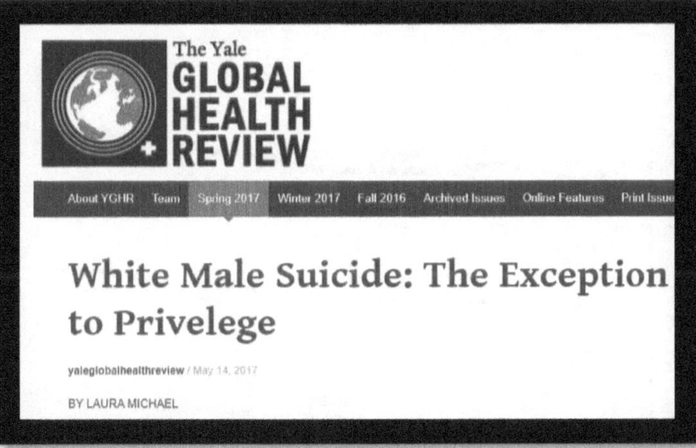

Figure 1. Age-adjusted suicide rates, by sex: United States, 1999–2018

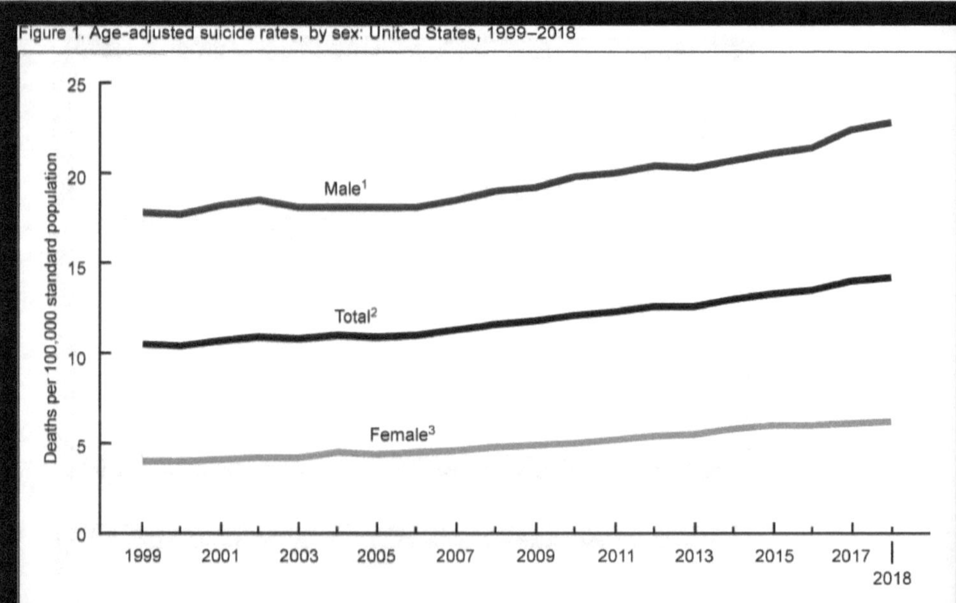

[1]Stable trend from 1999 to 2006; significant increasing trend from 2006 through 2018 with different rates of change over time, $p < 0.05$.
[2]Significant increasing trend from 1999 through 2018 with different rates of change over time, $p < 0.05$.
[3]Significant increasing trend from 1999 to 2015 with different rates of change over time; stable trend from 2015 through 2018, $p < 0.05$.
NOTES: Suicides are identified using *International Classification of Diseases, 10th Revision* underlying cause-of-death codes U03, X60–X84, and Y87.0. Age-adjusted death rates were calculated using the direct method and the 2000 U.S. standard population. Access data for Figure 1 at: https://www.cdc.gov/nchs/data/databriefs/db362-tables-508.pdf#1.
SOURCE: NCHS, National Vital Statistics System, Mortality (NVSS-M).

Suicide statistics

Learn the latest statistics on suicide. Data on suicide are taken from the Centers for Disease Control and Prevention (CDC) Data & Statistics Fatal Injury Report for 2018, as of March 1, 2020. Suicide rates listed are Age-Adjusted Rates.

Suicide is the

10th

leading cause of death in the US

In 2018,

48,344

Americans died by

Additional facts about suicide in the US

- The age-adjusted suicide rate in 2018 was **14.2 per 100,000 individuals.**
- The rate of suicide is highest in **middle-aged white men**.
- In 2018, **men died by suicide 3.56x more often than women**.
- On average, there are **132 suicides per day**.
- White males accounted for **69.67% of suicide deaths in 2018**.
- In 2018, **firearms accounted for 50.57% of all suicide deaths**.

The New York Times

Death Rates Rising for Middle-Aged White Americans, Study Finds

Angus Deaton with his wife, Anne Case, right, last month after he won the 2015 Nobel Memorial Prize in Economic Science. Together, they wrote a study analyzing mortality rates. Ben Solomon for The New York Times

By Gina Kolata

Nov. 2, 2015

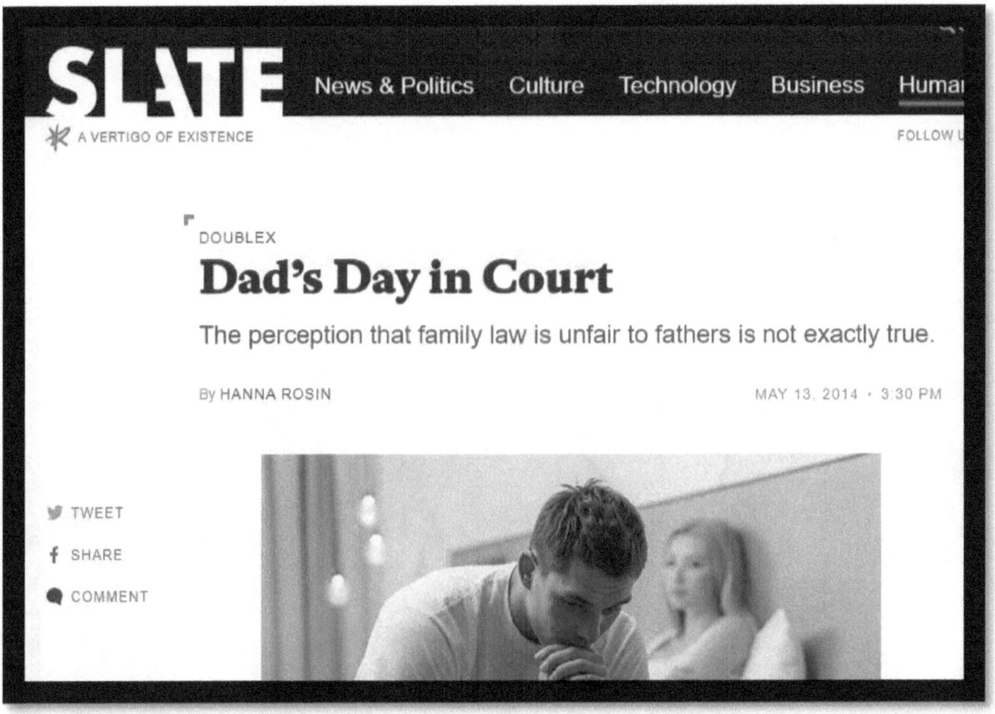

SLATE News & Politics Culture Technology Business Humai

A VERTIGO OF EXISTENCE FOLLOW U

DOUBLEX

Dad's Day in Court

The perception that family law is unfair to fathers is not exactly true.

By HANNA ROSIN MAY 13, 2014 · 3:30 PM

TWEET

SHARE

COMMENT

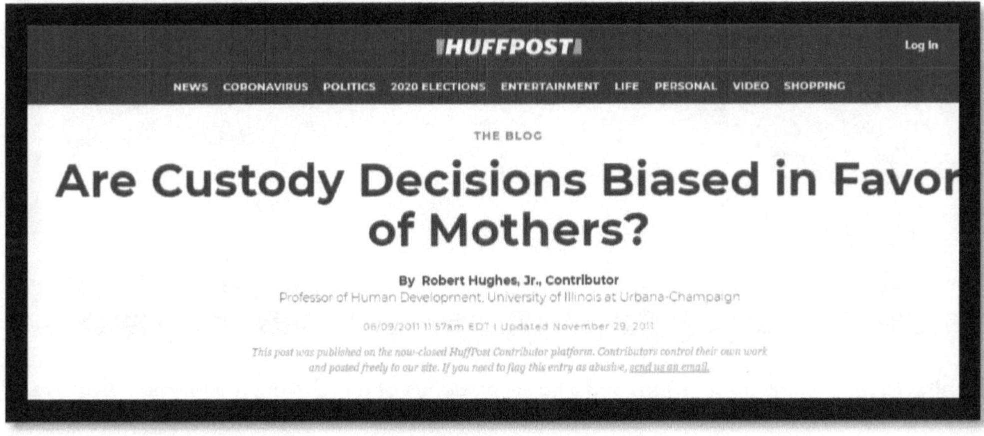

No sympathy - "They" (the "deep state") truly have restarted a "gender war" specifically targeting white men – If the "perception" is "not exactly true," then where does the "perception" come from and why are there so many articles published about the subject?

HUFFPOST Log In

NEWS CORONAVIRUS POLITICS 2020 ELECTIONS ENTERTAINMENT LIFE PERSONAL VIDEO SHOPPING

THE BLOG

Are Custody Decisions Biased in Favor of Mothers?

By Robert Hughes, Jr., Contributor

Professor of Human Development, University of Illinois at Urbana-Champaign

08/09/2011 11:57am EDT | Updated November 29, 2011

This post was published on the now-closed HuffPost Contributor platform. Contributors control their own work and posted freely to our site. If you need to flag this entry as abusive, send us an email.

(Is this honestly a question?)

(Ohhhh... I see... "Look at me, Mom and Dad – I actually got hired using my journalism degree!")

So they can therefore destroy the fabric of society making way for a Marxist nightmare.

(Uh-huh… sure – Does anyone truly believe that this could possibly be straightforward and objective reporting?)

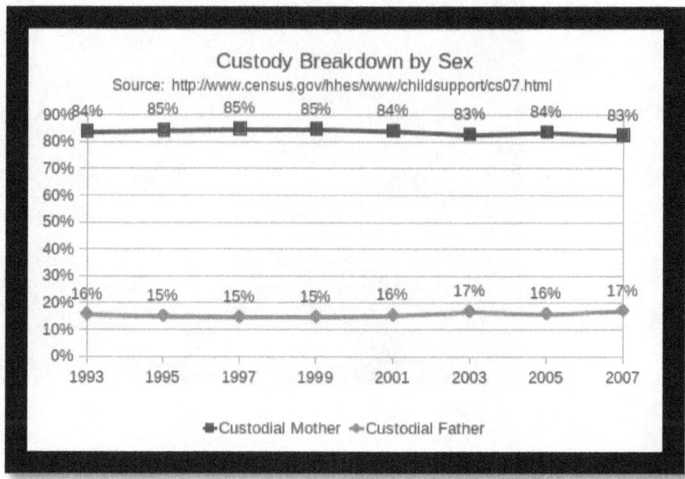

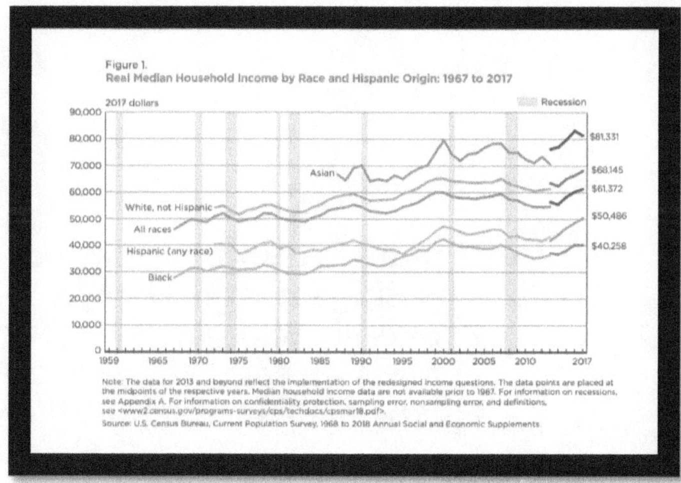

"N.E.S.A.R.A." & "The Great Awakening"

Updated: Trump Pushes For The Biggest Emergency Economic Stimulus in History — Mass Arrests, NESARA, Financial Reset Initiated?

03/17/2020 BY JUSTIN DESCHAMPS — 4 COMMENTS

NESARA

The National Economic Stabilization and Recovery Act

108th CONGRESS

2nd Session

H. R. ________________
(This bill has not yet been introduced into Congress)

To amend the Federal Reserve Act of 1913, as amended; and the Internal Revenue Code of 1939, as amended; in order to secure for the American people their unalienable right to Life, Liberty, and Property.

IN THE HOUSE OF REPRESENTATIVES

________________________ for himself, ________________________,

________________, ________________, ________________,

introduced the following bill; which was referred to the committee on

____

A BILL

To amend the Federal Reserve Act to provide for the American people a constitutionally accurate, sound, safe, and honest medium of exchange; and,

To amend the Internal Revenue Code enacted on February 10, 1939, as amended, to abolish the collection of revenue based on income and to establish a constitutional tax system within the classes of imposts, excises and duties;

So that the endeavors of the American people in agriculture, industry and commerce may prosper.

TITLE: NATIONAL ECONOMIC STABILIZATION AND RECOVERY ACT

Be it enacted by the Senate and House of Representatives of the United States of America in Congress Assembled,

Purpose

- To provide monetary reform by amending the Federal Reserve Act of 1913.
- To provide fiscal reform by amending the Internal Revenue Code of 1939.
- To secure for the American people their unalienable right to Life, Liberty, and Property.

What is wrong with America?

- The income gap between the rich and poor continues to widen
- Earnings for the poorest fifth of American families rose less than 1% between 1988 and 1998
- Earnings for the richest fifth of American families rose more than 15% between 1988 and 1998

- Income tax preparation costs Americans more than $225 billion and more than 5 billion hours per year in nonproductive labor
- Social woes and problems continue to escalate
- Income tax laws continue to erode privacy rights

- Asset forfeitures continue to rise due to inequitable monetary policy and tax laws
- The American Dream is quickly disappearing
- Unsound monetary and fiscal policies encourage waste and graft

- Public and private debt continue to rise
- Current banking practices and policies no longer support the people but special interests
- Current monetary and fiscal policy provides no mechanism to stop or defeat inflation

Can We Really "Fix" America?
Can One Bill Repair The Damage?

NESARA will:
- Reduce social inequalities and problems by doubling the average standard of living
- Eliminate trillions of dollars of public and private debt
- Return control of the currency to the public

- Reduces the cost of using public currency
- Provide new banking rules that are equitable and fair to all
- Provide $500 billion of new public works projects
- Replace the income tax with a fair tax

- Improve the balance of trade problems
- Rebuild American industry with high-paying, productive jobs
- Eliminate inflation

NESARA

The National Economic Stabilization and Recovery Act

Executive Summary

Monetary Policy Reform

- Establishes three types of United States currency: standard silver coin, standard gold coin and treasury credit-notes (*restores Constitutional currency*)
- The United States Treasury buys and cancels all outstanding capital stock of the former Federal Reserve Banks
- The privately owned Federal Reserve System becomes a public entity, the United States Treasury Reserve System
- A new Board of Governors of the Treasury Reserve System uses a specific law-mandated plan to maintain and stabilize the exchange value of the currency

- The new Board assumes all powers and responsibilities of the former Federal Open Market Committee
- The existing regional Federal Reserve Banks become Treasury Reserve Banks and continue clearinghouse operations and other bank service functions under the direction of the Office of the Comptroller of the Currency
- All commercial banks must exchange their income-producing government obligations for treasury credit-notes (*reduces the national debt*)
- Only treasury credit-notes may be held as bank reserves

- Fundamental changes are imposed on the repayment of all outstanding fractional reserve loans on secured property—principal must be repaid before the monetizing-fee is paid (*applies retroactively to existing mortgages reducing private debt*)
- A progressive federal excise tax is imposed on the privilege of making commercial loans of currency for profit
- Commercial financial institutions such as credit unions are provided, subject to some restriction, with opportunities to operate with fractional reserves

Fiscal Policy Reform

- Amends the existing federal income tax system
- A national retail sales (excise) tax is imposed upon non-exempt retail activities of commerce (*21 categories of exemptions covering most necessities of life*)
- The Internal Revenue Service is reorganized as the National Tax Service to administer the collection of the new tax

What NESARA Does Not Immediately Do

- Eliminate all payroll taxes, such as Social Security and Medicare taxes
- Eliminate constitutional excise taxes on regulated activities
- Immediately eliminate the entire national debt
- Immediately halt inflation (*the economy needs some response time before inflation will disappear*)

NESARA

The National Economic Stabilization and Recovery Act

Detailed Summary—Part I Banking and Monetary Reform

Immediate Relief and Results

- Eliminates approximately $1 trillion of the nation's public debt
- Reduces future private debt by approximately $1 trillion
- Immediately eliminates some private debt, especially for many homeowners

The Federal Reserve System

- The Federal Reserve Act of 1913 is amended
- The Federal Reserve System is abolished and replaced by a new Treasury Reserve System
- Control of the currency is moved from private control of the Fed to public control of Congress and the new Treasury Reserve System

- Congress sets the standards for the new monetary system but the people create as much or as little currency as they need
- Functions of the Federal Open Market Committee are transferred to the Board of Governors of the new Treasury Reserve System
- A new mechanism, the Treasury Reserve Account, is created to provide the Treasury Reserve System Board of Governors a better method to fine-tune the money supply, effectively eliminating inflation

- The Treasury Reserve System Board of Governors will continue using the previous three mechanisms for controlling the money supply: 1. Setting reserve requirements. 2. Setting the national discount rate. 3. Purchasing U.S. Treasury securities on the open market.
- All U.S. Treasury securities purchased by the Treasury Reserve System Board of Governors will be immediately turned over to the U.S. Treasury and cancelled out of existence.

Monetary Policy

- People are provided with several alternatives for currency
- Constitutional currency is restored
- Currency becomes debt free as the people stop paying interest payments for their use of a public utility

- Unlike previous policy, the new Treasury Reserve Board is provided one very specific mandate: maintain a stable currency
- Expansion of the economy is returned to the free market
- Private coinage is encouraged

- Exchange ratios for the various currencies are published at least weekly
- Printing of redeemable gold and silver certificates is allowed
- Postal money orders are made available in denominations of gold and silver coin

NESARA

The National Economic Stabilization and Recovery Act

Banking

- Returns the banking industry to serving public interests
- For secured loans, compound interest is outlawed and replaced with a monetization fee
- Provides stricter banking controls by imposing excise taxes to discourage high or runaway monetization fees

- On secured loans obtained from a fractional reserve bank, principal must be paid in full before the bank begins collecting its monetization fee
- Eliminates the façade for banking insurance (FDIC)
- Except for fraud and criminal activities, virtually eliminates bank failures

- Banks are prohibited from using as reserves any commercial paper
- Only Treasury credit-notes can be used as bank reserves
- Banks are prohibited from purchasing government issued debt, effectively removing banks from influencing monetary policy

- Checking accounts against gold and silver deposits are prohibited
- Commingling of funds among the various money accounts without owner's permission is prohibited
- All currency deposits with banks are general warrant deposits and custody accounts.

Detailed Summary—Part II National Sales and Use Tax

Immediate Relief and Results

- Workers maintain better control of their earnings
- Production is no longer taxed, just consumption
- Most of the necessities of life are not taxed

- Encourages production thus revitalizing industry in America
- Encourages rebuilding of inner cities
- Discourages wasteful uses of natural resources
- Exposes the true cost of government

- Greatly eliminates the struggle between tax "protesters" and bureaucracy
- Allows the "underground" to resurface and become a viable contribution to production of goods and services
- Greatly restricts the influence of special interests and lobbyists

The Income Tax

- The Income Tax Act of 1939 is amended
- People need no longer fear the IRS
- Billions of hours of nonproductive labor are eliminated

- Mounds of paper work are eliminated
- The cost of the income tax is no longer hidden and embedded in the cost of doing business and passed down the chain with the consumer paying the final tab
- Most likely eliminates state income tax plans because state income taxation piggybacks on federal income taxation

- The IRS is reformed into the National Tax Service
- Volumes of complicated tax code are history
- Eliminates personal income taxes

- Eliminates corporate income taxes
- Eliminates gift taxes and estate taxes
- Eliminates capital gains taxes

Sales and Use Tax

- Tax rate of 14%
- Government entities are exempt
- Government mandated expenses such as licenses, permits, passports, are exempt

- Sales of bullion, coin and currency are exempt

The National Economic Stabilization and Recovery Act

- Sales made by or to nonprofit schools are exempt
- Sales of prescription drugs, medical supplies and services are exempt

- Real estate rents and leases are exempt
- Sales of groceries are exempt
- Sales of plants, livestock and fish used in the production of food for human consumption are exempt

- Insurance sales are exempt
- Segregated portions of labor in retail service contracts are exempt
- Incidental or occasional sales such as garage or rummage sales are exempt

- Sales for the purposes of recycling are exempt
- Meals provided by companies at company expense are exempt
- Sales that are nonprofit in nature are exempt

SEVEN TRUMPETS
PROJECTED NEWS OF THE FUTURE

Chart columns numbered 1–7:

1 – 2	3 – 4	5	6	7
ANNOUNCEMENT OF CANDIDACY	CALM BEFORE THE STORM	STORM PHASE-1	STORM PHASE-2	STORM PHASE-3
CAMPAIGN & ELECTION	Q-ANON	MISSILE ALERT	STOCK EXCHANGE CRASH, US DOLLAR COLLAPSE REPLACED WITH USN	**SEVEN LAST COMMOTION**
MSM ATTACKS TRUMP	START OF COLLECTING SEALED INDICTMENTS	ASSASINATION ATTEMPT		1 — ABOLITION OF CIA, IRS, FEDERAL RESERVE
TRUMP INAUGURATED	MSM CONTINUE ATTACKING POTUS	MOUNTING & GROWING NUMBER OF INDICTMENTS	WORLDS CURRENCIES REVALUED	2 — IMPLEMENTATION OF NESARA / GESARA
				3 — INTRODUCTION OF ADVANCED TECH
		CALIFORNIA UNDER ATTACK	INDICTMENTS UNSEALED	4 — NEW FEMALE POTUS
			BEGINNING MASS ARREST	5 — RESTORED US REPUBLIC
		SPACE FORCE	FIRST BATCH TO GITMO	6 — GALACTIC FEDERATION MASS LANDING
		E.T. DISCLOSURE	UNCLOAKING OF GALACTIC SHIPS	7 — IT IS DONE!
		SOVEREIGN EXCHANGE		
2016	**2017**	**2018**	**2019**	**2020** *and beyond...*

Craft using an inertial mass reduction device

Abstract

A craft using an inertial mass reduction device comprises of an inner resonant cavity wall, an outer resonant cavity, and microwave emitters. The electrically charged outer resonant cavity wall and the electrically insulated inner resonant cavity wall form a resonant cavity. The microwave emitters create high frequency electromagnetic waves throughout the resonant cavity causing the resonant cavity to vibrate in an accelerated mode and create a local polarized vacuum outside the outer resonant cavity wall.

Images (2)

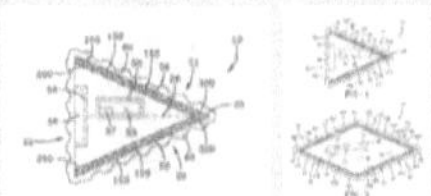

Classifications

- B64G1/409 Unconventional spacecraft propulsion systems

US10144532B2
United States

📄 Download PDF   🔍 Find Prior Art   Σ Similar

Inventor: Salvatore Cezar Pais

Current Assignee : US Secretary of Navy

Worldwide applications

2016 · US

Application US15/141,270 events ⑦

2016-04-28	• Application filed by US Secretary of Navy
2016-04-28	• Priority to US15/141,270
2016-04-28	• Assigned to DEPARTMENT OF THE NAVY ⑦
2017-11-02	• Publication of US20170313446A1
2018-12-04	• Application granted
2018-12-04	• Publication of US10144532B2

THE ★ WARZONE

Docs Show Navy Got 'UFO' Patent Granted By Warning Of Similar Chinese Tech Advances

Patent documents indicate that the U.S. and China are actively developing radical new craft that seem eerily similar to UFOs reported by Navy pilots.

BY BRETT TINGLEY AND TYLER ROGOWAY   JUNE 28, 2019

Texas Hill Country
NEWS   CITIES   ACTIVITIES   STORIES   SHOP   REAL
FACEBOOK / LENNY ZOO
LOCAL NEWS
The Truth About the Mysterious Tesla Tower in Texas
By Anna Hedges | December 12, 2018

Gaia
HOME   YOGA   MEDITATION   SERIES   DOCS & FILMS   TOPICS   NEW VIDEOS   EVENTS   ARTICLES
Articles > Seeking Truth > Secrets And Cover Ups > Forbidden Science
Massive Tesla Tower Suddenly Appears in Field Outside Waco, TX
Gaia Staff   September 24, 2019   3 min read

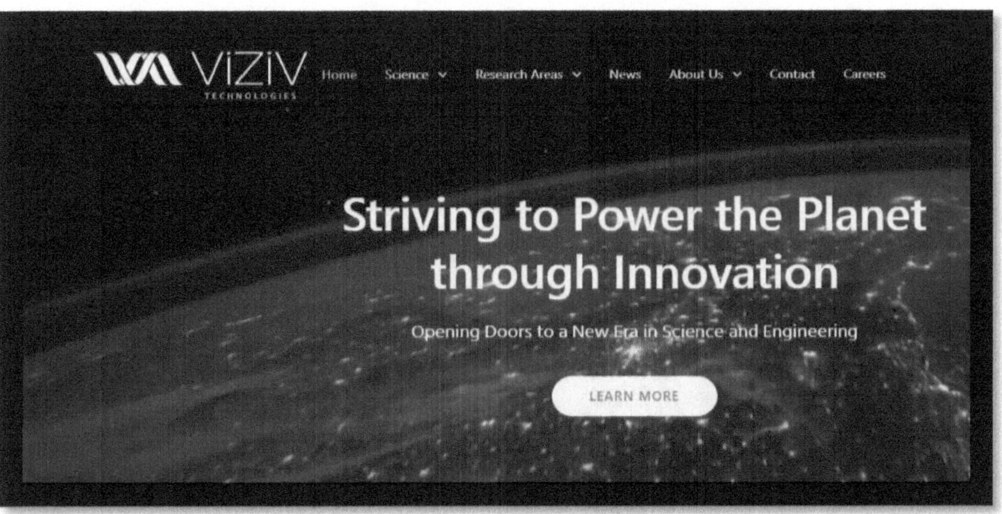

VIZIV
TECHNOLOGIES
Home   Science   Research Areas   News   About Us   Contact   Careers
Striving to Power the Planet through Innovation
Opening Doors to a New Era in Science and Engineering
LEARN MORE

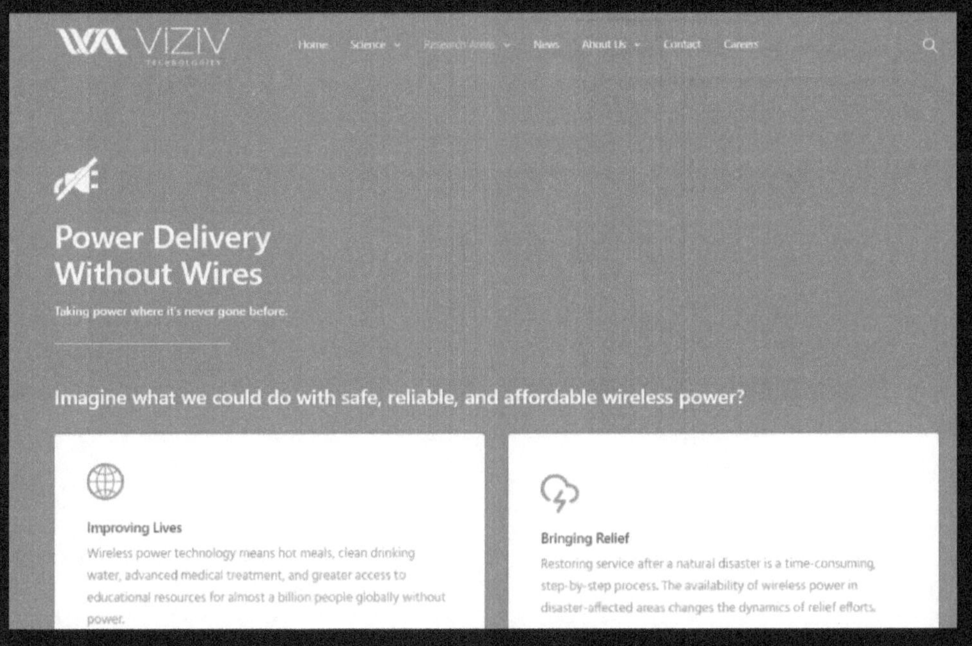

VIZIV
TECHNOLOGIES
Home   Science   Research Areas   News   About Us   Contact   Careers
Power Delivery Without Wires
Taking power where it's never gone before.
Imagine what we could do with safe, reliable, and affordable wireless power?
Improving Lives
Wireless power technology means hot meals, clean drinking water, advanced medical treatment, and greater access to educational resources for almost a billion people globally without power.
Bringing Relief
Restoring service after a natural disaster is a time-consuming, step-by-step process. The availability of wireless power in disaster-affected areas changes the dynamics of relief efforts.

T E S L A Life and Legacy - The Missing Papers

Home | Life and Legacy | Inside the Lab | Tesla for Teachers | Discussions | Resources

— The Missing Papers —

One of the more controversial topics involving Nikola Tesla is what became of many of his technical and scientific papers after he died in 1943. Just before his death at the height of World War II, he claimed that he had perfected his so-called "death beam." So it was natural that the FBI and other U.S. Government agencies would be interested in any scientific ideas involving weaponry. Some were concerned that Tesla's papers might fall into the hands of the Axis powers or the Soviets.

The morning after the inventor's death, his nephew Sava Kosanovic´ hurried to his uncle's room at the Hotel New Yorker. He was an up-and-coming Yugoslav official with suspected connections to the communist party in his country. By the time he arrived, Tesla's body had already been removed, and Kosanovic´ suspected that someone had already gone through his uncle's effects. Technical papers were missing as well as a black notebook he knew Tesla kept—a notebook with several hundred pages, some of which were marked "Government."

P. E. Foxworth, assistant director of the New York FBI office, was called in to investigate. According to Foxworth, the government was "vitally interested" in preserving Tesla's papers. Two days after Tesla's death, representatives of the Office of Alien Property went to his room at the New Yorker Hotel and seized all his possessions.

Dr. John G. Trump, an electrical engineer with the National Defense Research Committee of the Office of Scientific Research and Development, was called in to analyze the Tesla papers in OAP custody. Following a three-day investigation, Dr. Trump concluded:

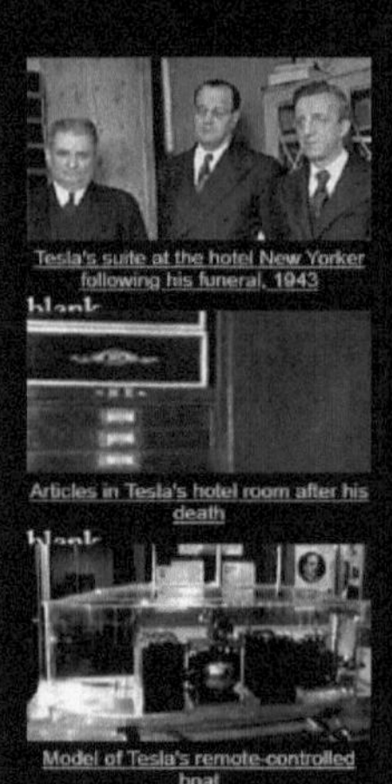

Tesla's suite at the hotel New Yorker following his funeral, 1943

Articles in Tesla's hotel room after his death

Model of Tesla's remote-controlled boat

> His [Tesla's] thoughts and efforts during at least the past 15 years were
> primarily of a speculative, philosophical, and somewhat promotional
> character often concerned with the production and wireless transmission
> of power; but did not include new, sound, workable principles or methods
> for realizing such results.

Just after World War II, there was a renewed interest in beam weapons. Copies of Tesla's papers on particle beam weaponry were sent to Patterson Air Force Base in Dayton, Ohio. An operation code-named "Project Nick" was heavily funded and placed under the command of Brigadier General L. C. Craigie to test the feasibility of Tesla's concept. Details of the experiments were never published, and the project was apparently discontinued. But something peculiar happened. The copies of Tesla's papers disappeared and nobody knows what happened to them.

In 1952, Tesla's remaining papers and possessions were released to Sava Kosanovic and returned to Belgrade, Yugoslavia where a museum was created in the inventor's honor. For many years, under Tito's communist regime, it was extremely difficult for Western journalists and scholars to gain access to the Tesla archive in Yugoslavia; even then they were allowed to see only selected papers. This was not the case for Soviet scientists who came in delegations during the 1950s. Concerns increased in 1960 when Soviet Premier Khrushchev announced to the Supreme Soviet that "a new and fantastic weapon was in the hatching stage."

Work on beam weapons also continued in the United States. In 1958 the Defense Advanced Research Projects Agency (DARPA) initiated a top-secret project code-named "Seesaw" at Lawrence Livermore Laboratory to develop a charged-particle beam weapon. More than ten years and twenty-seven million dollars later, the project was abandoned "because of the projected high costs associated with implementation as well as the formidable technical problems associated with propagating a beam through very long ranges in the atmosphere." Scientists associated with the project had no knowledge of Tesla's papers.

In the late 1970s, there was fear that the Soviets may have achieved a technological breakthrough. Some U.S. defense analysts concluded that a large beam weapon facility was under construction near the Sino-Soviet border in Southern Russia.

The American response to this "technological surprise" was the Strategic Defense Initiative announced by President Ronald Reagan in 1983. Teams of government scientists were urged to "turn their great talents now to the cause of mankind and world peace, to give us the means of rendering these nuclear weapons impotent and obsolete."

AMY DAVIDSON SORKIN

DONALD TRUMP'S NUCLEAR UNCLE

By Amy Davidson Sorkin
April 8, 2016

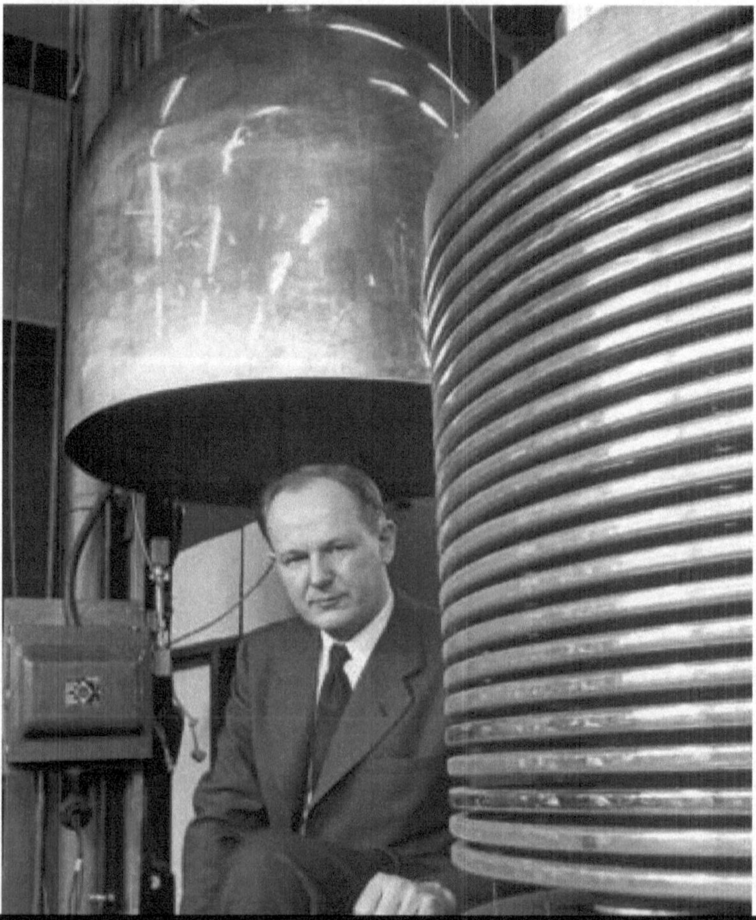

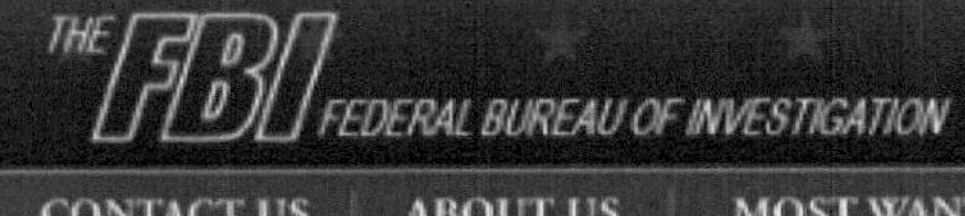

CONTACT US | ABOUT US | MOST WANTED | NEWS | STATS

Stories

Home · News · Stories · 2008 · July · FBI 100 - Top 10 Myths

Info This is archived material from the Federal Bureau of Investigation (FBI) website. It may contain outdated information and links may no longer function.

Twitter   Facebook   Share  

FBI 100
The Top Ten Myths in FBI History

07/24/08

For the past century, the FBI has been a vital player in American history, front and center in some of our country's most high-profile national security and criminal issues. Not surprisingly, some myths and misunderstandings about the Bureau have evolved over that time, in part because of the complex and sometimes sensitive nature of our work. We've picked out what we think are the top ten myths down through the years, leaving aside ones that are so fanciful that they don't deserve mention here...

In descending order, here they are:

Myth #10) The FBI has Nikola Tesla's plans for a "death ray"!

Nikola Tesla

If you don't know the name, Nikola Tesla was a prolific inventor and gifted physicist and engineer—most known for developing the basis for AC power—who was born in Croatia in 1856 and settled in the U.S. in 1884. When Tesla died in New York in January 1943, his papers—which were thought to include plans for a particle beam weapon, dubbed a "death ray" by the press—were temporarily seized by the Department of Justice Alien Property Custodian Office ("alien" in this case means "foreigner," although Tesla was a U.S. citizen). Despite longstanding reports and rumors, the FBI was not involved in searching Tesla's effects, and it never had possession of his papers or any microfilm that may have been made of those papers. Since 1943, we have told a consistent story to all who have asked. Reports to the contrary appear to be based on an initial confusion of FBI agents with other government officials—especially Alien Property Office personnel. These rumors have long been repeated in biographies and articles on Tesla without double-checking the facts as reported in our files.

Dr. Joel Wallach's Selenium Research Continues to Benefit Many

FDA Now "Urging" Selenium be added to Baby Food Formulas!

April 22, 2013 08:10 AM Eastern Daylight Time

SAN DIEGO--(BUSINESS WIRE)--Youngevity® Essential Life Sciences, a wholly-owned subsidiary of AL International, Inc. (OTC Pink: JCOF), announces that the research of Youngevity® founder, Dr. Joel D. Wallach, BS, DVM, ND, on Selenium continues to be at the forefront of health and prevention with the recent U.S. Food and Drug Administration (FDA) proposed rule requiring the addition of selenium to the list of required nutrients for infant formula products.

"may reduce the risk of certain cancers"

Tweet this

Dr. Joel Wallach has been at the front line of Selenium research for nearly 40 years. Selenium is an essential trace mineral that serves many functions in human physiology, including the synthesis of antioxidants (natural substances that neutralize free radical damage), and thyroid and immune function. In 2003, along with Youngevity®, Dr. Wallach successfully petitioned the FDA to establish a Qualified Health Claim for selenium adding that it "may reduce the risk of certain cancers" to labels of dietary supplements containing Selenium.

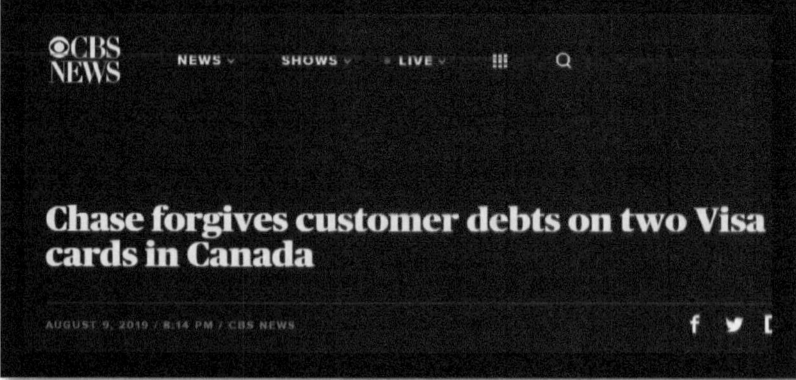

POLITICO

The idea of tying the dollar's value to gold has maintained popularity among groups with a strong distrust of the Fed — a camp that includes Judy Shelton, the president's latest pick for the Federal Reserve. | Andrew Harnik/AP Photo

FINANCE

Trump Fed pick's push for gold troubles lawmakers

Prominent economists agree that a return to a gold-linked dollar would not be better for the average American.

By **VICTORIA GUIDA** | 07/28/2019 06:57 AM EDT

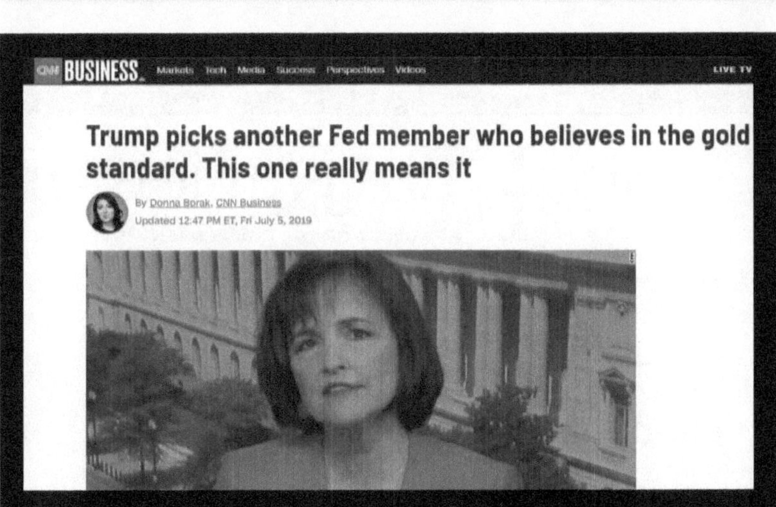

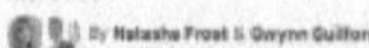

The quiet campaign to reinstate the gold standard is getting louder

July 3, 2019

By Natasha Frost & Gwynn Guilford

Crown of the realm.

The once-fringe fantasy of a return to the gold standard is creeping back into the mainstream.

It has long been dismissed as a fool's errand, on par with abandoning the Federal Reserve and other trappings of the modern economy. Mainstream economists deride it almost without exception. Reintroducing the gold standard would "be a disaster for any large advanced economy," says the University of Chicago's Anil Kashyap, who connects enthusiasm for it with "macroeconomic illiteracy." His colleague, Nobel laureate Richard Thaler, struggles with its very underlying principle: "Why tie to gold? Why not 1982 Bordeaux?"

Yet the idea that every US dollar should be backed by a small amount of actual gold is more popular than economists' opinions might suggest. Advocates include members of Congress and president Donald Trump. Enthusiasm for a return to the gold standard has become more prominent since Trump's most recent nominees to fill

FDAReview.org

A PROJECT OF THE INDEPENDENT INSTITUTE

Right-to-Try Legislation Helps Patient Battling Bone Cancer

By Raymond March · June 24, 2019

For the past several weeks the fake news media has been in an all out rampage against a chemical compound called chlorine dioxide (ClO2) and against me because I discuss the truth about it. This media barrage was started by Will Sommer for the Daily Beast in an article called "QAnon'ers Magic Cure for Coronavirus: Just Drink Bleach!" and the newswires spread it internationally. Promoters of this narrative inaccurately refer to ClO2 as an "industrial bleach" and label me as a YouTube conspiracy theorist who "promotes drinking bleach to cure everything." Nope. Not. At. All. That's why we call them the fake news after all, right? And if you think the news is fake, imagine how fake their science is! Media attacks against this chemical compound and those who talk about it are nothing new. This article will discuss what chlorine dioxide actually is, some of my personal experiences with it, and the misrepresentation that our media and Pharma owned medical "authorities" give us on the subject.

SO, WHAT IS THIS STUFF? IS IT ACTUALLY BLEACH?

Let's start with basic semantics. By designating something that has the ability to decolorize and sanitize as a 'bleach' is confusing a process with a product. A verb instead of a noun. For example, lemons can bleach, the sun bleaches, but we don't necessary label those as 'bleach'. And just like lemons and the sun, ClO2 can also decolorize and sanitize, and is used industrially to do so, but this doesn't make it harmful for humans in every capacity. Whenever a media or science talking head states that ClO2 is "essentially bleach," either they didn't pass high school chemistry or they're knowingly misguiding you—trying to confuse people into thinking it's the same as the commercial Clorox tucked away in our laundry cabinets. Clorox bleach itself is sodium hypochlorite, which of course, is not chlorine dioxide, and has far different mechanisms of action. And what's funny is that Chlorine dioxide is a gas, so when the media says "drink bleach" they're just further revealing their ignorance. So as you can see, there's a total misrepresentation of what ClO2 actually is—a gaseous compound that works to disinfect pathogens very effectively through oxidation.

CHLORINE DIOXIDE KILLS HARMFUL BACTERIA?

Yes. ClO2 kills bacteria, viruses, cancer cells—it will selectively target anaerobic pathogens and kill them through oxidation, an electrical reaction where one chemical steals the electrons of another. Some in the health community may be familiar with the oxidative capacity of food grade hydrogen peroxide and ozone therapy, chlorine dioxide oxidizes similarly. When a ClO2 molecule comes into contact with a virus or bacteria cell, it rips electrons from the cell and destroys it. Because of its sterilization ability and relative cheapness, this compound is commonly used in a variety of industries such as hospitals and restaurants. The Environmental Protection Agency has it registered for these purposes. However, ClO2 isn't just used as an industrial cleaner, a stabilized version is commonly used by hikers and campers to kill waterborne pathogens for clean drinking water. These potable water drops and tablets have chlorine dioxide listed as the main ingredient and can be easily purchased at any camping supply store such as REI or online shopping websites like Amazon. So, if chlorine dioxide is not a "toxic bleach," why are people like myself being ridiculed by mainstream media for discussing it? And why is there no mention of suppliers like REI and Amazon? Two reasons—one is simply shoddy and the other is downright shameful. Shoddy journalism is to blame when only the biased FDA is used as a resource. For example, the FDA puts out warning letters about ClO2, calling it a deadly bleach without explanation, citing zero science or research about the compound. Yet, the military and the EPA use ClO2 at high dosages to tackle extreme contaminants like Anthrax and Ebola, and the USDA and even the FDA itself have chlorine dioxide registered to decontaminate with. And take a look at this—studies have been done showing chlorine dioxide to be effective at killing the coronavirus too. Take that, propaganda peddlers! And it goes to note that while high dosages of most decontaminates are not safe to be around, low doses (like what hikers use for potable water and those drinking it internally to kill pathogens) can be very safe. Anything can harm or help depending on how you use it. Conscious usage is key. And the shameful part of this issue? The medical establishment is trying to suppress the sharing of any potential health benefits of ClO2 because it is inexpensive and effective.

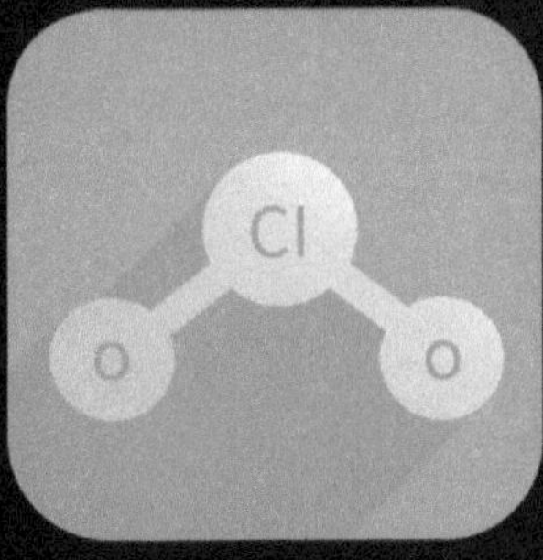

WHAT DOES ALL THIS HAVE TO DO WITH MMS?

Some folks who have used and taught about chlorine dioxide for health-supporting purposes call it the "master mineral solution" and "miracle mineral supplement" or MMS for short. I prefer to call it what it is—chlorine dioxide, because it removes any preconceived notions. It's not magically "miraculous," it's just reality! The most notable proponents of MMS are Daniel Smith of *Project Green Life* and Jim Humble, who has been heavily denigrated by Big Pharma. In 2015, Smith was sentenced to 51 months in federal prison for (basically) teaching too many people about MMS. You can find/support him at standbydaniel.com. And Humble is attacked routinely by the press even though, as his name suggests, he's a very humble man. His resources are incredibly helpful in understanding chlorine dioxide protocols and can be found on his website https://jimhumble.co. A helpful resource for information on ClO2 is an "MMSWiki" page that highlights Humble's research in a Wikipedia style format. And on a side note, Wikileaks released an email regarding MMS/chlorine dioxide in their 2012 *Global Intelligence Files* data dump. It consisted of public disclosure for a number of internal emails between the employees and clients of Stratfor, a geopolitical intelligence company. For some reason, a private company that works with the intelligence community on information analysis, Stratfor, had collected an email on MMS. I find that intriguing. You can read that email here. And before YouTube censors any of them, check out these interviews with European professional Andreas Kalcker. They are top notch!

HOW IS MMS INFORMATION BEING SUPPRESSED?

Due to the viral nature of social media and with so many people waking up, information about MMS has become widespread. The FDA has attempted to counter with two press releases. The first in 2010 was then rereleased in 2019, entitled: *"FDA warns consumers about the dangerous and potentially life threatening side effects of Miracle Mineral Solution."* This from the FDA—a financially motivated agency that racks up millions in user fees per year (as part of their Prescription Drug User Fee Act), has approved deadly drugs like opioid painkillers, and only approved 'medical marijuana' after a man-made pharmaceutical version was created.

In April of 2017, I released a short 4 minute video about MMS on my *Destroying the Illusion* YouTube channel and in just over a year it had amassed 250,000 views. It was ranked #1 on YouTube's search results for "MMS." Consequently, YouTube started censoring my video from searches and in May of 2019, they completely removed it and added a strike to my channel. This was followed by a targeted media blitz against MMS led by *Business Insider* and other media outlets during the summer of 2019, culminating in the FDA warning letter. See how they operate? Censor the truth beforehand, then publish smears and lies afterward so no one can search for any real information. Then, once they print that it's a dangerous-deadly bleach and claim people were harmed, the FDA is "forced" to take action. Information warfare.

> "SEE HOW THEY OPERATE? CENSOR THE TRUTH BEFOREHAND, THEN PUBLISH SMEARS AND LIES AFTERWARD SO NO ONE CAN SEARCH FOR ANY REAL INFORMATION. THEN, ONCE THEY PRINT THAT IT'S A DANGEROUS-DEADLY BLEACH AND CLAIM PEOPLE WERE HARMED, THE FDA IS "FORCED" TO TAKE ACTION. INFORMATION WARFARE."

SO HOW DOES SOMEONE FIND AND USE IT?

I personally don't sell it, but there are still some active vendors as well as a few different ways to make your own ClO2 gas. An easy way to make it is by combining sodium chlorite and citric acid solution in a small 1:1 ratio of drops in a clean glass and allow 30-60 seconds to activate. That's pretty much it. When mixing the drops, it's commonly referred to as 1 "drop of MMS/chlorine dioxide" when 1 drop of sodium chlorite is added to 1 drop of citric acid. 1+1=1 drop MMS. Easily dispensable bottles of sodium chlorite and citric acid can be purchased online at kvlab.com. Now, let's discuss when to take these drops and how many. One of the more well known (but intensive) regimens is Humble's Protocol 1000, whereby one would take 3 drops of MMS (3+3) every hour for 8-12 hours a day. With a protocol like this where a small amount of ClO2 is getting into the blood for a prolonged period of time, it allows the compound to do more work on the pathogens in the body. If it were only taken twice a day, even in higher amounts, it still wouldn't be in the body as long. I have never done this protocol myself and I rarely use MMS in general these days, but I have the bottles and the knowledge on hand, just in case. What I have done in the past are "maintenance doses" of 5-10 drops of MMS once or twice a day. I've also used chlorine dioxide gas to help clear and cleanse my sinuses and respiratory tract by gently inhaling, holding, and exhaling for a few repetitions. An important warning about using ClO2 is the "Herxheimer Effect", named after the doctor who first studied it. Essentially, if the body detoxifies too fast, it can cause nausea, stomach distress, or diarrhea. As such, it's important to start slow when detoxing the body.

HOW DID I DISCOVER ALL THIS?

In 2011, I became acquainted with an individual who had medical experience but was fed up with the establishment medical system. He decided to continue helping people through natural modalities. After he taught myself and some of my colleagues about MMS, we spent a few years experimenting with it—both cleaning and using it internally. One of my favorite experiences with MMS was when I met a woman with stage 4 ovarian cancer. She refused chemotherapy and successfully healed herself with a modified regimen of MMS and the Gerson Therapy.

HOW DID I DISCOVER ALL THIS?

In 2011, I became acquainted with an individual who had medical experience but was fed up with the establishment medical system. He decided to continue helping people through natural modalities. After he taught myself and some of my colleagues about MMS, we spent a few years experimenting with it—both cleaning and using it internally. One of my favorite experiences with MMS was when I met a woman with stage 4 ovarian cancer. She refused chemotherapy and successfully healed herself with a modified regimen of MMS and the Gerson Therapy.

CONCLUSION

Be aware that many organizations have special interests and will cite their own sources to promote a particular narrative. You can believe what the fake news and fake science would have you believe, or you can research for yourself and put their narratives to the test. I've always found there to be no better teacher than personal experience. No source can surpass the knowledge you've gained from witnessing something first hand. The more knowledge you have from your research and experiences, the more you will know the truth of what's really going on in the world, and how to manage any circumstances that may arise. I don't refer to anything as a "cure," for truly there are no cure alls. I don't believe in banking on one compound or pill to be our savior, which is why I don't refer to chlorine dioxide as "magic." Instead, I believe that we should be looking holistically at ourselves to figure out how we can practice prevention or to keep a situation from progressing. There are many powerful substances that are cheap, safe, natural, and readily available that can be used as part of this holistic regimen. It is only through our own ignorance that we don't know how to use them, let alone realize they exist. We must undo the mass programming. Knowledge is power.

12 BAD FOODS

by Dr. Peter Glidden

Wheat

Barely

Rye

Oats

Corn

Soy

Meat with nitrates

Oil in a bottle

Carbonated drinks with a meal

Well done red meat

Fried food

Baked skins of potatoes/yams

Latest Issues

THE SCIENCES   MIND   **HEALTH**   TECH   SUSTAINABILITY   VIDEO   PODCASTS   OPINION

HEALTH

What Are ORAC Values?

Nutrition Diva: Quick and Dirty Tips for Eating Well and Feeling Fabulous

By Nutrition Diva Monica Reinagel on August 14, 2013

ORAC stands for Oxygen Radical Absorbance Capacity. It's a lab test that attempts to quantify the "total antioxidant capacity" (TAC) of a food by placing a sample of the food in a test tube, along with certain molecules that generate free radical activity and certain other molecules that are vulnerable to oxidation . After a while, they measure how well the sample protected the vulnerable molecules from oxidation by the free radicals. The less free radical damage there is, the higher the antioxidant capacity of the test substance. There are actually a handful of different tests designed to measure total antioxidant capacity in this way, but the ORAC is probably the best known and most popular.

The nice thing about this method is that it measures the antioxidant *activity* of a food rather than the levels of specific nutrients, such as vitamin C or E. After all, there are thousands of unique antioxidant compounds in plants, most of which we haven't even discovered yet.

2450 

A Beautiful Brave New World Lies Ahead

Q !!mG7VJxZNCl 7 Nov 2018 - 11:12:06 AM

We are going to show you a new world.
Those who are blind will soon see the light.
A beautiful brave new world lies ahead.
We take this journey together.
One step at a time.
WWG1WGA!
Q

Q Clearance Patriot

Anonymous 1 Nov 2017 - 8:56:16 PM

Q Clearance Patriot

My fellow Americans, over the course of the next several days you will undoubtedly realize that we are taking back our great country (the land of the free) from the evil tyrants that wish to do us harm and destroy the last remaining refuge of shining light. On POTUS' order, we have initiated certain fail-safes that shall safeguard the public from the primary fallout which is slated to occur 11.3 upon the arrest announcement of Mr. Podesta (actionable 11.4). Confirmation (to the public) of what is occurring will then be revealed and will not be openly accepted. Public riots are being organized in serious numbers in an effort to prevent the arrest and capture of more senior public officials. On POTUS' order, a state of temporary military control will be actioned and special ops carried out. False leaks have been made to retain several within the confines of the United States to prevent extradition and special operator necessity. Rest assured, the safety and well-being of every man, woman, and child of this country is being exhausted in full. However, the atmosphere within the country will unfortunately be divided as so many have fallen for the corrupt and evil narrative that has long been broadcast. We will be initiating the Emergency Broadcast System (EMS) during this time in an effort to provide a direct message (avoiding the fake news) to all citizens. Organizations and/or people that wish to do us harm during this time will be met with swift fury — certain laws have been pre-lifted to provide our great military the necessary authority to handle and conduct these operations (at home and abroad).

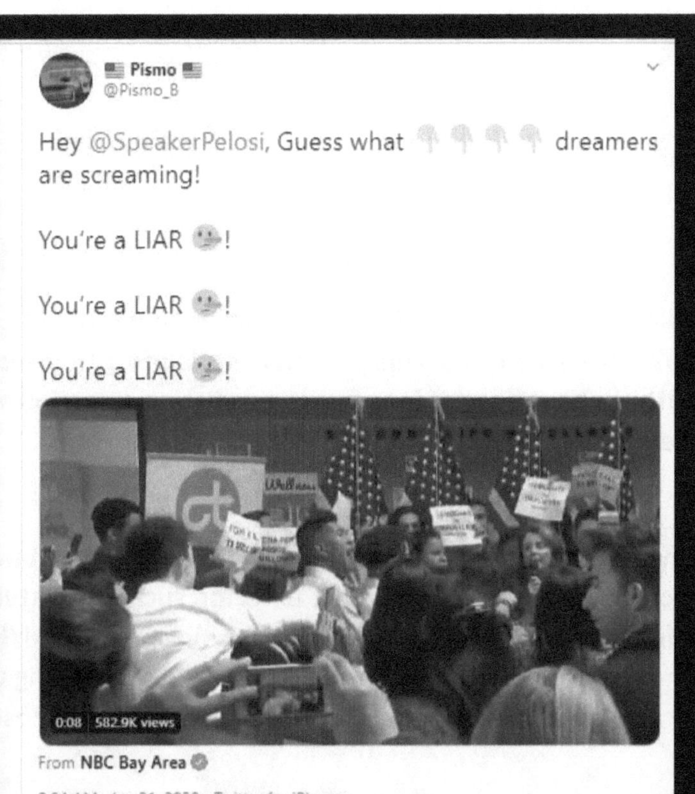

Pismo
@Pismo_B
Hey @SpeakerPelosi, Guess what dreamers are screaming!
You're a LIAR !
You're a LIAR !
You're a LIAR !
0:08   582.9K views
From NBC Bay Area
9:04 AM · Jan 31, 2020 · Twitter for iPhone

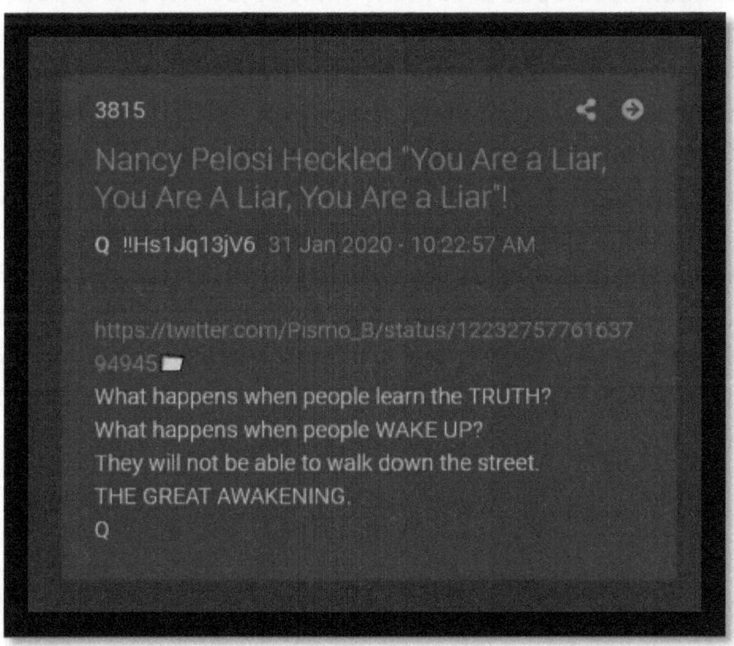

3815
Nancy Pelosi Heckled "You Are a Liar, You Are A Liar, You Are a Liar"!
Q !!Hs1Jq13jV6 31 Jan 2020 - 10:22:57 AM
https://twitter.com/Pismo_B/status/12232757761637
94945
What happens when people learn the TRUTH?
What happens when people WAKE UP?
They will not be able to walk down the street.
THE GREAT AWAKENING.
Q

It Is What It Is

It can be a challenge to face some of the information that has been presented within this book – The strategy of this particular style of writing and organizing information within a book format is as much a stylistic expression as it is a functional necessity.

In a similar way that the architect Louis Henry Sullivan designed buildings with the structural components revealed on the exterior, such is this style exposing the structural integrity of the information that is being presented (bibliography, footnotes) as having a foundation in truth according to supporting sources recognized as carrying a credible voice, as much as that may be possible "these days."

This style has been developed over many years of journalistic experience as well as interaction with the "general public" regarding these subjects – In a similar way that a design of a vehicle may be assisted by the use of a "wind tunnel" in order to maximize efficiency, similarly I have experienced a "wind tunnel" of sorts in the form of blind outrage directed in my general direction from sharing some of this information, true as it may be – In an attempt to present this information with the creation of a minimum amount of outrage, I am quite literally "blaming the messengers" by utilizing an obsessive amount of media citations under the protection of "Fair Use," for indeed I believe that this book will make an excellent addition to any academic curriculum involved with the truth, the law, politics, history, the future and, perhaps, journalism.

George
not just politics as usual
GOOD NEWS:
LIVE FOREVER!
LOVE YOUR
JOB!
BILL GATES
TALKS TO JOHN KENNEDY
ABOUT MURDOCH,
MONEY, AND WORLD
DOMINATION
CAN
POLITICALLY
INCORRECT'S
BILL MAHER
MAKE IT IN THE
BIG TIME?
EXCLUSIVE:
THE INSIDE STORY OF
JIMMY CARTER'S
FINAL DAYS IN OFFICE
INDICTMENT DAY:
WILL HILLARY
GET BUSTED?
CARL SAGAN'S
FAREWELL
ADDRESS
THE END OF
SOCIAL SECURITY:
WHAT'S BROKEN AND
HOW TO FIX IT
SURVIVAL GUIDE TO THE
FUTURE
So we hope you enjoy George's take on the
future. Why not put it in a safe place somewhere
and take it out in 20 years? To paraphrase a
great Englishman, it may not get you what you
want, but you just might find, it will get you
what you need.
John Kennedy
PLATFORM 2020
NO POLITICIAN EVER LOST A VOTE
BY INVOKING THE FUTURE. YOU
KNOW, OUR CHILDREN DESERVE
A BETTER ONE, AND BILL CLINTON
IS BUILDING A BRIDGE TO A
BRIGHTER ONE. IT'S THE MOST
OVERUSED WORD IN THE POLITI-
CAL LEXICON, YET DETAILS ARE,
AS USUAL, SPARSE. WHAT DOES
THE FUTURE HOLD? A NEW WORLD
OF PROMISE OR APOCALYPSE? WE
LAUNCHED A DISCOVERY MISSION
TO THE NEXT MILLENNIUM TO
FIND OUT WHAT'S ON THE OTHER
SIDE. SO BUCKLE YOUR CHIN
STRAP AND HOLD ON AS GEORGE
ENTERS THE TIME WARP AND RE-
EMERGES IN THE YEAR 2020
PLATFORM 2020
A SURVIVAL GUIDE TO THE FUTURE

Bush Is Smart Enul by Richard Reeves · Best of Rock & Politics
George
The
Secret Behind
Trump's Political
Fling

Who's ready for the Trump Rally tonight?
#WWG1WGA
erictrump • Follow
erictrump TULSA OKLAHOMA HERE WE COME!!!
25m
brendakoski @ususus #TrumpRally
34s Reply
jt92kelly Does this mean what I think it means...
30s Reply
yoshiopath You have no real friends. Think about that.
9,189 likes
25 MINUTES AGO
Log in to like or comment.

Ancient Hebrew letter Q over Washington DC last night.

(Thank *YOU*, President Trump!)